THE IDLE TRAVELLER

THE ART OF SLOW TRAVEL

A good traveller has no fixed plans
And is not intent upon arriving
Lao Tzu, Tao Te Ching

THE IDLE TRAVELLER

DAN KIERAN

AA

Published by AA Publishing, a trading name of AA Media Limited, Fanum House, Basing View, Basingstoke, Hampshire, RG21 4EA, UK. Registered number 06112600.
www.theAA.com

First published in 2012
10 9 8 7 6 5 4 3 2 1

A CIP catalogue record for this book is available from the British Library.

ISBN: 978-0-7495-7342-3

Jacket design by Mark Thomson
Illustration by Chris Wormell
Typeset by Servis Filmsetting Ltd
Printed and bound in the UK by Clays Ltd

A04779
Our books carrying the FSC label are printed on FSC certified paper. FSC is the only forest certification scheme endorsed by the leading environmental organisations.

Contents

Foreword

This book is dedicated to my two children, Olive and Wilf. At the time of writing, Olive is 18 months old and she loves to take me out for walks as often as she can. She makes me put on her shoes, puts on her coat and then walks up to the front door, tapping it with her finger. 'Dar!' she says, over and over again, until we head out, hand in hand, to explore the world. Sometimes we stay a few metres from the front door, playing with the moss growing on the wall. Other times she breaks free and runs, squealing, to the bottom of the road. Once we went up and down the escalators in our local department store 15 times. I always let her lead the way, though. For half an hour she's in complete control.

There is something about going for a walk with a toddler that baffles and inspires me at the same time. For one thing, you have no idea where you're going. It can be rather annoying because it seems such a long-winded way of doing things, but very quickly you learn to relax and find meaning in the experience. There are no boxes to tick. It is utterly purposeless and yet, once you've got through the self-important rage that descends when you're forced to let go of the haste of normal life, it teaches you truths about yourself you had no idea you longed to know.

The idle traveller is just like that toddler – ambling out into the world at the whim of their own curiosity, searching for meaning and following whatever sparks their sense of adventure along the way.

Dan Kieran

Introduction

by Tom Hodgkinson

Idleness and travel do not, on first sight, make the most obvious bedfellows. The idler is by nature a stay-at-home sort of person, a fireside loafer who might perhaps prefer to travel through antique lands, through the medium of maps and books, rather than go to the trouble of actually travelling. As Pascal wisely noted: 'All of man's troubles come from his inability to sit still in his own room.' Leave the house and your troubles start. The very word 'travel', we are told, derives from a word meaning 'three-pronged instrument of torture'.

And yet, and yet... despite the obvious inconveniences of travel, the idler can be stirred to leave his room. The idler is also a wanderer, a meanderer, an observer of life, and some of the greatest idlers have also been the greatest travellers, and travel writers. I think of the constitutionally indolent Dr Johnson, who would lie in bed till noon every day, but took a spirited and sometimes arduous journey to the Highlands of Scotland in the company of young Boswell. Another example would be Robert Louis Stevenson, who wrote beautifully in praise of idleness, in an essay produced when he was 26, but who was also a traveller. His *Travels with a Donkey* is a masterpiece and he is perhaps the strongest influence on one of our greatest contemporary travel writers, Paul Theroux.

So travel and idleness are more closely connected than you might think. Perhaps it would be more accurate to say that the idler has a revulsion for that form of commodity which is sold as travel these days, by which I mean the holiday. Not that we would criticise tourism *per se* – after all, it is pleasant to wander aimlessly through an Italian city-state, or to lie on a hot beach near water. But there is perhaps something unsatisfying about the holiday in the sun, as the Sex Pistols pointed out many moons ago. It is a fantasy, and an expensive one at that. It is a slave's reward, a consolation prize for those trapped in a boring job.

We could say the same of that over-used word 'experience'. Instead of embarking on the difficult project of living well, we instead tend to choose a life of boredom in work, punctuated by hi-octane 'experiences' that are to be ticked off from a list. We have all seen those 'One Hundred Things to Do Before You Die' features in – magazines. Drive a Ferrari, go to Royal Ascot, do the Dakar rally, attend the Cannabis Cup in Amsterdam and so on *ad nauseam*. Sadly Dave Freeman, who invented the concept, died at just 47.

I first met Dan Kieran when he popped into the office of *The Idler* magazine, which was then located in Camden Town. We gave this cheerful chap a task to do and he kept coming back to help out. Gradually he became more enmeshed in *The Idler*, and was deputy editor for many years. We used to have great fun in the office and we had many philosophical discussions; I flatter myself that Dan's years at *The Idler* helped to frame the philosophical attitude that went on to inform this book.

What Dan has attempted in this book is to outline a particular philosophy of travel, where travel becomes part of one's own therapeutic journey, rather than simply an escape. So it would be true to say that idle travel does not mean comfortable travel or easy travel. In fact, Dan reserves particular ire for the soul-deadening effect of fancy hotels. It is not even necessarily slow travel, for the actual pace of movement is surely relative – a train ride would have seemed impossibly fast to a Florentine apothecary of 1450. Idle travel is nothing to do with 'fun' in the modern sense, meaning a temporary escape from our ills. No: it is more to do with attitude. Perhaps 'deep' travel would be a better synonym.

Now, just as a little work is acceptable as a sort of condiment to the idleness which follows it, so a tough journey makes the pleasure of arrival all the sweeter. I think a love of ease needs to be mixed with a stoic acceptance that the road will not always be easy. I remember going on a really arduous and lonely train ride from northern Germany to a Greek island when I was in my early twenties. Having got most of the way, I was sitting in a little port with absolutely no idea how to get to my destination. I asked around but received only shaken heads in reply. I gave up. I sat down on my bag and put my head in my hands. I abandoned all hope. At that moment, a little boy came up to me: 'Mister, mister, the bus for Lefkas leaves in 20 minutes.' I got on the bus and arrived at my destination, a beachside café called Paradise. The owner brought me a beer. I sat down, gazed at the water and was overcome by inexpressible joy. Idleness is always sweet, but when it is richly deserved, it is all the sweeter.

Perhaps the greatest form of idle travel is the solitary walking tour. It is here that you can discover true freedom at low cost, and indulge in that forgotten pastime: thinking. Much of today's travel is expressly designed to prevent thought. Airports are not conducive to calm reflection. Their hideously bland architecture instead presents you with myriad distractions from contemplation in the form of screens, shops and announcements. You can never really relax, or be in the moment. Walking, on the other hand, gets you back in touch with the self. Hazlitt's lovely essay, *On Going A Journey*, has the following lines:

> Give me the clear blue sky above my head, and the green turf beneath my feet, a winding road before me and a three hours' march to dinner – and then to thinking! It is hard if I cannot start some game on these lone heaths. I laugh, I run, I leap, I sing for joy.

Walking is liberty and, by the way, the walking does not need to be done in the countryside. Our great cities are wonderful for walking. When I visit London, I will quite often take an hour-long walk from Bayswater to Pimlico, and meander through Hyde Park, alongside the Serpentine and across Sloane Square. What a rich selection of sights I see, and how much thinking I get done. And while walking I like to think of myself as a *flâneur*, that species of meandering poet who loved to stroll through 19th-century Paris at a snail's pace. Walter Benjamin said of the *flâneurs* that they liked to take a tortoise on their strolls, because that ponderous creature would set the right pace. Robert Louis Stevenson argued that solo walks are best:

> Now, to be properly enjoyed, a walking tour should be gone upon alone. If you go in company, or even in pairs, it is no longer a walking tour in anything but name; it is something else and more in the nature of a picnic.

Well, a picnic is no bad thing, but we get the point.

It's a shame that the train has been invaded by mobile phones, laptops and on-board screens, because train travel used to provide a blessed break from work and distraction. Now you can carry on your business from the train, or watch telly on it, when before you only really had two choices: read or stare out of the window, both of which are idle pleasures. I'm so sorry; there is of course a third: dozing. Trains, unlike cars, encourage napping. Of course it is possible to disconnect from the machines on a train, and we should perhaps discipline ourselves to switch off the mobile phone and leave the laptop in the luggage rack.

The book that you are about to read is based on Dan Kieran's 20 years of idle travel. His slow travel adventures began as a result of his fear of flying. He was forced to find alternatives, and that is precisely what introduced him to what it really means to travel. He's now very grateful to his fear, for without it he would never have discovered slow travel at all. This has not always made his life easy. (And we should re-emphasise here that 'idle' is not a synonym for 'easy' or 'comfortable'. In fact, the desire for idleness, or call it freedom, can often make life very difficult indeed.) While Dan's friends hop on a plane to Poland for a wedding, he has to take the train there and back. His journeys can be arduous. But he will at least feel alive while travelling; he will at least meet people; he will hear stories and see sights that are hidden to the aeroplane traveller.

Yes, Dan really does walk the walk. One of his great slow travel escapades was the month-long jaunt across Britain in a milk float with two friends that he recounts in this book. The point really about this journey was that it connected him with other people. How many times have you met someone in an airport and struck up a conversation? The experience de-alienated Dan: he found that far from what newspapers might make you believe, this country is full of helpful people. Community is by no means dead.

The Idle Traveller is perhaps more than anything a song in praise of the unplanned, of letting go. Modern travel, in particular the modern holiday, tends to be carefully structured to a timetable. Activities are built into each day. We have an itinerary, a coach trip, a sightseeing tour. Even those who have paid to be in their holiday resort will joke that they are in Colditz. But, as Dr Johnson had it: 'nothing is more hopeless than a scheme for merriment'. Planned fun rarely lives up to the hype, and Dan is very good on the feeling of deflation that, for example, planned sightseeing can leave you with. Children may like these holidays because there is lots of 'fun' to be had in the form of waterslides and all the rest of it. And this sort of holiday may have its place for families: Dan doesn't mention the fact that, as well as being an idle traveller, he is also a fan of Center Parcs. However, we cannot really say that such holidays are anything to do with travel. They are just a little break.

No. The best nights out and the best travelling 'experiences' are often the unplanned ones: the chance encounters, the kindness of strangers, the accidental discovery.

As I said, no one ever said idle travel was easy. There are many touching accounts of disastrous experiences in this book: particularly painful is the story of Dan's many faux pas with his son Wilf in the freezing cold public baths of Budapest. Dan's solution is to ensure he always has a good book to hand: not a conventional guidebook, but a piece of literature related to the area he is visiting, or a relevant biography. Thus travel for Dan incorporates extended reflections of a literary and philosophical nature. Idle travel, then, is the opposite of escape – it is an 'inscape', if we can invent a word for intensive but productive inward thought.

Let us also say that idle travel has much more in common with the old-fashioned pilgrimage than with the fun-packed suspension of toil of the modern holiday. Whether taken alone like Christian in *A Pilgrim's Progress*, or in company like the pilgrims of the *Canterbury Tales* (which sounds like the most fun holiday ever), it is a spiritual journey. The pilgrimage is designed to help you to grow as a person, to help you to reconnect with yourself and with others, to heal yourself of trauma. In a word, it is therapeutic.

This is the sort of travel hymned by Austrian writer Stefan Zweig, who emerges as one of Dan's literary heroes. Zweig, born in 1881, remembers a world where speed, one of our modern gods, was thought to be unrefined and vulgar. So it is idleness that can help us to become noble once again, to unplug from machines and to immerse ourselves in chaos and nature. One of the most beautiful parts of this book is Dan's account of being with golden eagles. Idle travel, Dan argues, can help us to reconnect with the wild places, those places that the bourgeois world attempts to close off.

Above all, idle travel, we might even say 'real' travel, awakens the poet and the philosopher within. We are all philosophers, but the myriad cares of modern life tend to make us forget this fact as we seek distractions from our pain rather than facing up to it. As my friend Penny says, when you take a painkiller, the pain is still there, *you just can't feel it.* We all apply sticking plasters to our lives in the form of booze, drugs, affairs, card games, various addictions, holidays, luxury hotels and travel 'experiences' in our efforts simply to cope. But the idle traveller, for better or for worse, rejects the sticking plaster and goes on a journey into the soul. If he glimpses hell on the journey, so be it. He will glimpse heaven as well. And after the long and arduous climb, the view will be superb.

Chapter 1

Travel, don't just arrive

Hey man, slow down.
Radiohead, The Tourist

Like most people, I only feel I'm really travelling once I've left the airport far behind. Trains to London from Chichester, where I live, go via Gatwick. A familiar feeling of expectation builds as we pass through Horsham, Crawley and Three Bridges. At first it's impossible to tell which of the passengers around me will be getting off at the airport. Then I start to spot the vast suitcases, and as we get closer people begin to fidget. I see them biting their nails while staring anxiously at the list of stations that shunt across the dot-matrix screen. The business travellers come into focus at the same time. They reveal themselves with a sudden flurry of phone calls. They talk with bravado of their high-flying trip, lured into a glamorous portrayal of what will surely be a tedious sales conference in a business park near a provincial airport. After hanging up, they turn towards the window with a loud sigh, their disappointment manifesting itself as condensation on the glass.

Soon after that I can hear the tinny white noise of a jet engine. It becomes so loud that the nervous holidaymakers stare into the middle distance with a mix of shock and awe. The men in suits exhale loudly. People start to grumble about the security searches while checking for the umpteenth time that their passport is in their flight bag. Then there's a flurry of movement as everyone collects their bags and suitcases.

As they disembark, the passengers begin losing their heads, like animals sensing the approach of a hurricane. The businessmen try to appear above it, but bundle through the chaos with a careless shimmy all the same. On the platform suitcases battle for supremacy for the lift, but there's already a line of people from the last train waiting for it. Finally the last bag is dragged off. The doors beep and close, and the carriage pulls away.

Everyone has made it on to the platform. Everyone, that is, except me. I never get off at the airport. It's only when Gatwick is in the distance that I know I'm really on my way.

***

Like millions of other people from the UK who travel to Europe every year, I was heading for the Mediterranean coast of Spain. Unlike those millions of people, I was getting to Marbella by overnight train.

I haven't been inside a passenger aeroplane for over two decades, preferring to travel everywhere by land or sea. This fact has been deemed quaint enough to warrant many holiday-article commissions from various national newspapers over the last ten years. *Newsweek* was once even moved to call me the 'Champion of Slow Travel'.

Slow travel has been drifting in and out of fashion for a decade, almost always pegged to some kind of environmental press release. This is something I find rather strange. I do consider myself to be respectful to planet earth – I recycle and try not to waste water – but the real reason I travel the way I do is simply that it's more interesting and fun. What's more, if I'm not travelling slowly, I feel I'm not really travelling at all.

Obviously you have to fly to *some* parts of the globe, but 80 per cent of the trips people in the UK make abroad are to European destinations. It amazes me that so many of those trips are taken by air. Aeroplanes are extraordinary things, but there's no doubt in my mind that journeys began to be seen as a chore, something to mutter about under your breath or an ordeal to be endured, with the arrival of the cheap flight and the package deal. This brings us to an uncomfortable truth about the modern holiday. Paradoxically, now that we can move so quickly around the world, most of us don't actually travel any more – we only arrive.

At Victoria Station in London I bought a few provisions for my first-aid kit and then got in a black cab to take me to St Pancras, where I would take the Eurostar. I was booked on a sleeper train from Paris to Madrid that evening, with a rail connection to Marbella the following morning. Sitting in the cab I began to feel a little sneaky, as though I were bunking off school. All those people going by air would now be in an unnaturally lit waiting room filled with the bars and boutiques of boredom. They had stopped travelling and become a piece of cargo, to be frisked of their money in a departure lounge before being sifted, weighed and deposited in a small seat on the aeroplane. They would soon have their bodies searched for guns, bombs and knives, while those with babies would have to prove that any bottles of expressed breast milk were not concealing nitroglycerine by taking a quick swig.

Of course many people are very happy to be transported in this way, despite the delays, security searches and the mad scramble for seats if they're travelling with a budget airline, but the fact remains that for the duration of the journey their mobility will be restrained and their brains fed recurring and familiar images and films on a small screen. After a few hours of this they'll be delivered to another airport. Now that the world is punctuated by global brands, homogenising the grammar and ideas that structure our lives, someone who moves from their Western home via an airport/shopping mall into an aeroplane that shows them their favourite Western TV shows and then drops them off at another airport before a taxi takes them to a hotel – itself selected because it provides Western food and entertainment – certainly achieves movement. But you begin to wonder if they've really gone anywhere at all.

Airport departure boards seem to cheat you with their functionality, too, while the ones at railway stations awaken my imagination. I always find myself daydreaming about the people I could have been and the lives I could have lived.

At St Pancras I made my way through the security screen and 25 minutes later I was gliding towards Paris. The Eurostar is where the romance of adventure begins to claim me. I lived in London for many years and always found the possibility of escape on long-distance trains intoxicating. I now realise that the city was where my attitude to 'slow' or 'idle' travel first began to evolve in an entirely unpremeditated way.

***

I moved to London when I was 21 and stayed there until I was 33. I'd been nervous about the move, having grown up in a small town in rural England. One day, in an attempt to find my own sense of place in the vast and seemingly impenetrable city, I decided to avoid the underground and use only the bus.

When you take the tube you get from A to B very quickly. It's undoubtedly efficient and much more practical when it comes to getting to and from work, but it is utterly hopeless when it comes to developing any sense of place. I soon realised why I'd found London so daunting as a tourist. I had snippets of memories of disparate places that had no obvious link. London to me was a mash-up of postcard pictures, each surrounded by – well, that was the point – nothing at all. The news, with its stories of crime-ridden chaos, left the London of my brain flitting between terror and tourist cliché. All its magic and history seemed to be drowned out by the ruddy-faced Beefeaters, pickpockets and Royals who no doubt, after a tough day posing for photos, put their feet up together in the Hard Rock Café.

Obliterating this perception on my bus journeys allowed me to discover the city in a way that wasn't just practically useful, it changed my attitude to living in London entirely. Lots of people said I was mad wasting so much time on the bus when I could just have embraced the pace of the metropolis by using the ultra-efficient tube, but I never looked at it that way. I enjoyed taking my time to walk round the periphery and through all the parks and began to piece together the way one part of London ended and another began; I found seemingly forgotten corners and shadowy streets that filled out the parts in between. I even picked up a sense of the contours that cities do such a good job of hiding.

'Get a map, you fool!' I hear you cry, but maps are little practical use without a landscape and a sense of place to enjoy them through. After a year or so I began to feel much more relaxed in whichever part of the city the tube now took me to. Soon I understood the street map intuitively without having to look at it. The city – even one as vast and marauding as London – had finally become my home.

I now apply this principle when I travel anywhere. I always take the slower route if I can, because it gives the journey and the places I visit a much greater sense of meaning than I'd experience by flying over the sea – however much more efficient that may be. Most importantly for me, travelling slowly changes the way my mind interprets the world, and in this book I'll explain how slow travel can make you think differently too.

***

Hearing the French language on the Eurostar adds to my sense of relaxation – as though I'm being culturally acclimatised by the journey. Exactly the same thing happens geologically if you're prepared to take your time. Kent and northern France become connected in your mind, as they once were by a bridge of land our ancestors must have walked across thousands of years ago. It's only a different kind of electricity pylon and cars on the wrong side of the road that give the country away. Travelling slowly picks at the fabric of national identity, as boundaries between nations are revealed as the transitional ideas they are. Arriving in a city by train, rather than aeroplane, also changes the way you feel about your destination. Gare du Nord introduces you to the city in a way that's much closer to the way a local sees it. Rougher around the edges, perhaps, but exciting, not daunting, and it's much easier to blend in and slip away. Who and what you are remains deliciously undefined.

The contrast with air travel is stark. Land at Charles de Gaulle Airport and you'll find yourself pigeon-holed immediately. You'll be bombarded with adverts, brochures and offers positioning you as a tourist whether you like it or not. Before you know it you'll unconsciously be *thinking* like a tourist, too. You've only just landed, but already you've been turned into an economic statistic to be converted into euros in exchange for the trinkets that have been developed especially to target you.

I left the station among domestic travellers and within moments I was blending in with commuters crossing the Seine. I just made out the back of Notre-Dame through the window of the Metro before being deposited on the steps of Gare Austerlitz in the evening sun. Gare Austerlitz is where the Ellipsos Trainhotel for Madrid leaves every night at 7.45pm. It's a 900-mile journey that takes 13 hours and costs from £100 return. If you're feeling flash, for £700 return you can get a Grand Class cabin for two that has its own shower cubicle. You also get dinner in the restaurant car with unlimited wine along with a cooked breakfast the next morning as part of the fare.

The passengers queuing for the Ellipsos Trainhotel have changed over the years – they've got much younger. You still find plenty of well-dressed old ladies, inter-railers and a few relaxed-looking suits, but now you see lots of young families too. It really is a magical way to travel, but don't take my word for it. The average occupancy for the service is 87 per cent – all year round. If you want to go in the summer or during school holidays you need to book up to three months in advance, but that's the best time to get the cheapest tickets. If you time it right (and you buy your ticket from Deutsche Bahn's UK call centre), you can get combined first-class tickets for your whole journey wherever you're going across Europe for the price of a ticket on an airline.

The sense of expectation and excitement is mixed with nerves to begin with – missing an overnight train on your own or especially when you have young children with you can be a bit grim – but once aboard and safely settled in your cabin those anxious faces morph into a collective grin. You're welcomed onto the train by an attendant who takes your passport (so you aren't woken up when you cross the border into Spain); they also ask what time you'd like the seats of your cabin to be turned into bunk beds in the evening and offer to book you in for dinner in the restaurant car. My son's favourite part of any holiday is always the 'sleeping train' wherever we happen to go. It must be the combination of unusual snacks, bunk beds and a different kind of screen to stare through. There's also no concept of bedtime. Everyone settles into an individual rhythm. Mum and Dad get a break because little children can't run off anywhere and get into trouble. Occasional trips to the restaurant car are fun, especially as the evening draws in, but you are delightfully self-contained in your cabin, allowing you all to relax in a way that's impossible on an aeroplane.

This time I was sharing with people I didn't know in a standard bunk in a four-berth couchette. I was first into the cabin and as my travelling companions appeared we exchanged polite smiles. A heavily tattooed man drinking a can of lager and an unrelated boy of around 15 or 16 arrived after me. The boy looked nervous and immediately began to fumble with his hand-held computer screen. The older man offered me a can of beer. I took it and showed him four of my own under my seat. He laughed as I offered one of mine to him, accepted it and leaned back growling something before slapping my knee repeatedly. It's always a good move to have some way to break the ice with strangers in a couchette. Not for reasons of security, as you might think, more for your own sense of relaxation. Exchange smiles and a few words early on and you'll find yourself much calmer in their company as the journey progresses. Often you get students on their own inter-rail adventure and they almost always speak English, which is convenient if a little shaming. Having garbled conversations with strangers is all part of the fun, though. It's incredible how much you can learn from gestures, facial expressions and exuberant pointing.

I looked around the couchette. It was old and slightly grizzled but well tended and clean. The beds had not been set up yet and you could feel the three of us willing the concierge to come and fold our seats away. Just before the train left Paris he arrived. We all shuffled into the corridor and I heard the familiar drawl of young Americans a bit further down the carriage. I've seen many young Americans on overnight trains over the years, but hardly any young Britons. Once our beds had been prepared – snug green blankets tucked over white sheets with a bottle of water and complimentary wash bag – a Frenchman in his late 60s emerged and looked grumpily at his ticket and the top bunk bed it related to. (You can specify a top or bottom bunk when you book and it's always easier to move around if you are on the bottom.) It took three of us to lift his vast suitcase up onto his bed only for him to leave immediately, waving a packet of cigarettes as he went back out onto the platform. We didn't see him again until the following morning.

I woke up at six the next day while the others were still asleep in the bunk to my left and the one above.

The train lolloped along, making the 'clack, clack' sound that had put me to sleep seven hours before on our way through France. In another life the cabin would have seemed small for a prison cell, but this enclosed space allowed my mind to wander. Lying there as we lurched along, my memory drifted back over 20 years of slow travel. I have no idea how many night trains I have now been on, but I vividly remember the first. Fourteen hours from Venice to Prague in 1994.

I was inter-railing with my friend Henry and we spent the night scrunched up on the floor of the coach corridor, taking it in turns to stretch our legs into the open door of the leaking toilet's cubicle. We spent a month journeying across Europe: hitchhiking through France, Italy, the Czech Republic and Holland and taking in Florence, Prague and Amsterdam. Back then the allure of a night train was slightly more practical – it allowed you to wake up in a new country without having to pay for a bed for the night. We had very little money and no real clue about what we were doing apart from a few tourist boxes we hoped to tick. I was clear on one thing, though: I knew I would be a different person when I got home.

Without photographs on hand in my Trainhotel bunk, I watched the mental video clips of that first trip from my memory instead. One string of images always demands to be recollected before any other. We were walking along a country road somewhere south of Lyon. It was early and hot. The campsite we were heading for was 10 miles away. Our rucksacks were heavy with all the things we had thought we would need before we had any idea what they might be. We were hitchhiking with a few francs, a road atlas that was utterly useless in the scale of real life and no plan B should things go awry. In those days mobile phones were heavier than a house brick and found only on bankers with red braces, so we were totally alone and out of contact with the world. The asphalt was dusty, the ground scorched by the early September heat. We had water, but I could tell it wouldn't be enough. In the absence of parents, and feeling slightly homesick, I became compulsively responsible. I think Henry felt it too. We kept feverishly applying sun cream onto the back of our necks as we plodded along in silence. We were a long way from home and a mere 72 hours into our adventure. I remember the pang of sheer terror as we stared out at the unknown. The threat of defeat and returning early taunted us every time something failed to live up to our grandiose expectations.

We stopped at a crossroads and had to guess which way to go. We sat on our rucksacks and drank some of the water we had left. I rolled myself a cigarette. There were no cars to give us a lift. We dozed for a while in the shade and then the panic arrived when our last drop of water ran out. But the more fervent the fear became, the more I found myself able to look through it. Now that the worst had happened – we were stranded in the middle of nowhere on a boiling hot day with no water and no idea where to go – I was strangely comforted by something I had never experienced before. My shoulders relaxed. We both began giggling and finally worked out that this feeling was exactly what we'd come looking for. We had found genuine escape and for the first time in our short lives had an inkling of what that word actually meant. Freedom from responsibility, and more pressingly with an empty vista where a career should be on the horizon, liberation from expectation of the lives and the people we would one day become.

Eventually we found a main road and started to hitch less earnestly. Now in fits of laughter we decided to try the *Sure Thing* method from the John Cusack movie. At one point the main character gets down on his knees and literally begs cars to stop. Henry told me I was mad, but as soon as we both did it someone stopped for us and we were on our way. The battered car was small and the interior had been pulled apart. I sat in the front seat and managed a short conversation with the driver, probably only a few years older than we were, and learned the car was made in 1975 – making it the same age as me.

The reflections and feelings that filtered through my mind in the couchette were far truer than the photos I took when we were there. Those pictures show a slightly nerdy and skinny young man wearing sunglasses on his head and biting his nails, but I recall a youthful T E Lawrence, pushing himself and discovering a new outlet for his curiosity and sense of adventure. I never look at photographs if I want to remember a time I went travelling. The most important parts of any trip – how you felt and what you learned – only seem to collect in your mind many years later. If it was truly important, you'll remember it. You may not understand *why* the thing you can remember is valuable when it seemed less crucial at the time, but that realisation will come eventually.

Incidentally, I think this is why looking at other people's photographs from their own travels can be so tedious. All the things that they can see in their minds, the experiences they are rapturously trying to reveal to you, aren't in their photos either. I find photographs break the spell that will happily grow and morph in your brain as you age and your recollections begin to change. Trying to fix these moments in a frame is like trying to turn a park bench back into a tree. If you're lucky or a photographer, it might become an artwork in and of itself because of the light or the way it's composed, but it contains none of the magic it held when it actually used to *be*.

***

A few hours later the train arrived at Chamartin Station in Madrid. We were two hours late and there was a slight danger I'd miss my connection south to Malaga. I'm usually very careful to allow for delays when I book a connection – sleeper trains into Spain and Italy are often late – but this was a last-minute work trip I'd been rather rushed into. I am the CEO and co-founder of a website called unbound.co.uk and I was heading down to Marbella to meet a potential investor. My two other co-founders were coming to the same meeting, but they were taking a plane.

It took a few minutes to consult an iPhone app I'd downloaded to help me negotiate the Metro and that resulted in the right ticket and the right line. The Madrid Metro, like the Paris one, seemed incredibly flimsy compared to the London Underground, with large roomy carriages and little silver handles that flounce open the bouncy doors. I had to go 16 stops to the Atocha Renfe station and enjoyed people-watching on the way. There were lots of immaculately attired old ladies and commuters, but not the monochrome suits you'd get in London around the same time of day.

Foreign railway stations offer you as many metaphors as they do destinations. I'm sure that comes from the mindset of travelling – for some reason you begin to ponder ideas and questions that never appear in quite the same way when you're using public transport at home as part of your daily routine. My favourite metaphor came alive when I hurried to make my connection to the coast. Rather like the process of life itself, lone travellers like to think they are on some kind of grand mission that only they understand. It's where my mind goes while I am between point A and point B that often excites me more than my destination. Now I found myself literally walking against the flow, becoming a rock for the tide of commuters and briefcases to froth around. Every shirt and tie that poured around me seemed unconscious, as I looked around bemused, trying to find the right platform for my next train. I stopped to absorb the scene, as I always do. If you find yourself heading in the opposite direction to most of the people around you it's usually a sign you're going a more interesting way.

In the middle of the flow I saw a life preserver in the

form of a red jacket and a beautiful blonde woman wearing a badge that said 'Can I help you?' in various languages. She smiled and pointed my way. I jogged up some stairs and shoved my bag into the x-ray security machine. A long escalator gradually took me down to the train and I found my seat with minutes to spare. The air conditioning was welcome, as was the speedometer that excited the small boy inside me. The high-speed Talgo trains (known as 'Ducks' because of their bill-like nose) travel at up to 200 miles an hour and take two and a half hours to get to Malaga on the coast, via Cordoba, where you can change for Seville. Similar trains run in Germany and if you book a seat in the first carriage you can enjoy the driver's view, because there's only a glass panel between you and what they can see. That's not for the faint-hearted, by the way.

The only downside with Spanish trains is their habit of having a film playing on TV screens that are visible wherever you happen to sit. Headphones are handed out from a little basket before you leave, so you can listen in. I turned to the other screen and watched the edges of the city give way to fields, trees and dusty roads. The railway-carriage window is surely the original TV.

***

My first solitary slow travel experience was again related to Henry. I took the train from London to Warsaw in Poland to be best man at his wedding 10 years after we'd hitched through Europe. It was to be an eventful journey. From London to Brussels, Brussels to Cologne and then a sleeper train over the border into Poland. It turned out to be a triumph of serendipity and completely liberating in that a terrorist attack scuppered all my careful planning before I'd even walked out of my front door. I watched the news over breakfast and discovered that a mortar had been fired at the MI6 building from the railway line all the Eurostar trains had to run through. The mortar had no effect on the MI6 HQ, but it totally obliterated my schedule. Rather like the feeling of panic that dissipated at that crossroads in the French countryside when my worst fears were confirmed, the discovery that my microscopic itinerary had been utterly ruined made me feel strangely calm. Then I felt that sense of excitement building again. I was about to have another adventure.

All the other wedding guests had flown from London to Warsaw in a few hours and as the celebrations drew to a close a few days later, I found my earlier tube and bus analogy holding true in the bar of the hotel. I felt different in a way I was unable to explain to the people around me. I kept recalling the changes in landscape, architecture, language, facial expression, music, manners and fashion I'd experienced along my journey through the heart of Europe. I had met incredible people, many of whom helped the desperate young man from London whose journey had been blown apart by the IRA. I saw commuters in Belgium, Germany and Poland and marvelled at the way work has uniformed all our lives. I was full of questions and unfamiliar thoughts and feelings. I felt slightly outside myself for most of the way. When I finally arrived at Warsaw Central Station, I was terrified by the vast and intimidating Soviet structure that threatened to crush me, but my journey came to an abrupt end in a different way – with an overpriced taxi ride to my four-star Western hotel. Even though I was in Warsaw, the taxi and the hotel room suddenly seemed reassuring, but in a totally false way. The convenience and familiarity repelled me. I longed for the journey when I'd felt different and had accessed a different part of 'me'.

Paul Theroux recently said in an interview for the *Guardian* that travelling is best done alone. There are certainly no more compelling travelling companions than the inescapable thoughts and feelings of your own soul. Travel with a friend and his or her presence secludes you from the way your brain delves into itself when you are in an unfamiliar place and wholly alone. When you travel alone your identity slips away, especially if you do it slowly and go a long way. You speak very little, which in itself is quite meditative. Your thoughts are free to roam into the often-neglected parts of yourself. The transition can be uneasy at first, but soon there is great comfort in what is lost.

Back in the bar in Warsaw I looked around my friends differently. They were utterly unchanged by having moved a short space across the globe. They talked about the same things we talked about at home: music, politics, old friends, problems at work and things in the news. There was no evidence they were being influenced by different thoughts or ideas. Their journeys had been an efficient means to an end. A chore to be endured between home, the wedding and then home again. Their lives had barely been interrupted at all.

That was not my experience. My mind was all over the place. I was roaming parts of myself I was usually far too busy to notice. I felt as though I would never be the same again. No part of my brain was still in London. Every scrap of me was right there. I longed to get out of the hotel and to keep going. The next day a few of my friends dropped me off at the station for my long journey back to London. They would fly out that night and be home in time for *News at Ten*. I still had 24 hours' travelling to go. They looked at me in a kind, but slightly baffled way. One of them called me eccentric as they waved goodbye, but I was filled with a kind of nervous glee. I was feeling scared, but at the same time I couldn't wait to be on my way. An hour later I got talking to a Russian soldier who was sharing my cabin and had, it transpired, deserted his post and was on the run. While talking to him I imagined my friends 35,000 feet up in the air watching re-runs of American TV shows and I knew I would never travel that way again.

***

At Malaga Station I got a train to the airport, where I would meet my two friends and business partners, Justin Pollard and John Mitchinson, who had flown in that morning for our meeting. I was early and it was already very hot. Outside the airport, queues of gleaming white buses waited for the holidaymakers the flustered reps in bright uniforms were trying their best to collect together. The tourists looked uneasy, becoming more relieved as they took the short walk between air-conditioned airport and air-conditioned bus and had the first glimpse of what they'd come for – the sun. John and Justin emerged, both very smart in off-white cotton suits, and greeted me with hugs and warm grins. Philosophically, I think they are both with me on the whole slow travel thing, although I'm sure they find the practicalities a little eccentric. We went on to have an excellent few days in a castle overlooking Marbella with our potential investor, though the money remained untapped by the time we all set off for home.

After waving goodbye to the others at the airport I went down to Marbella itself to walk along the famous golden mile on my own before heading off on my long journey back to Britain. Marbella is a classic destination for British tourists. Guaranteed hot weather and the hope that the glamour provided by a plethora of actors, footballers and celebrities might rub off on the rest of us are part of the attraction that entices many to holiday here. Malaga Airport is only 30 minutes away and Malaga itself is a mere two and a half hours by air from London.

Marbella is, I have to say, a very odd place. The hills behind the town are festooned with lavish houses in gated communities that look down on golf courses. Lots of Premiership football teams and the England squad come here to train, but beyond the golf courses the glamour stops abruptly. There's a huge motorway with a scar of neglected development between the exclusive hillside properties and other palatial homes by the sea. I'm sure one day the builders will move back in, but when I visited it looked full of damage and decay.

The beach itself is nice but pretty unremarkable. Nowhere near as beautiful as West Wittering's, near to where I live, though the weather is considerably better. You get palm trees and on a clear day the north coast of Africa gives you a sense of exoticism that rather shames the golden mile itself. Nothing here is left to the imagination. Everything that could conceivably be attractive has been packaged and exclusivised in such a way that you can consume whatever you want without any need for individual search or discovery.

Eventually my feet brought me to the edges of Puerto Banus, a marina where people park vast motorboats that I suspect rarely get used. In front of the boats you'll see Ferraris and Rolls-Royces squeezed into parking spaces and behind them the standard luxury shops you find in places where the fantastically wealthy choose to live. Beyond the gin palaces, as my Dad calls them, you eventually come to the beach bars and clubs that appear every season in the pages of *Hello!* and *Heat* magazines. Ocean Club Marbella is raised up on a kind of white stage a few hundred yards from the beach, inviting – no, demanding – that you stare at the beautiful bodies parading across the boards. Hiring a sunbed to lounge on can cost hundreds of pounds for the day. A review on TripAdvisor around the time I was there claims the staff are sometimes rude if you don't spend enough money, telling one visitor: 'People don't come here to eat sorbet, they come here to drink champagne.' The review continues: 'It's pretentious, takes itself way too seriously and is full of people who need to prove they have money.'

Over the years, as a travel writer often sent on holidays for free, and usually receiving a daily rate of expenses paid by the travel company (around £50 a day), I've spent a bit of time in five-star hotels that I could never afford to stay in normally. I've only ever paid to stay in one once, and that was Claridge's in London, but whenever I find myself in this kind of place I always take the barman to one side and ask about the clientele. Every single one of them has told me a variation of the same thing: 'The people who can afford it are fine. It's the ones who can't that are a nightmare.'

You can imagine it, can't you? You scrape together enough cash to stay somewhere fabulous, having been bamboozled by the online brochure, only to find it doesn't live up to your expectations, so you end up spending a fortune *and* having a miserable time. Personally I can't stand madly expensive and exclusive hotels. I appreciate the 'It's all right for you getting in for free, I'd love to do that' argument, but they really are totally ghastly after a few days, even when you're not paying. Perhaps precisely *because* you're not paying, as it's only then, paradoxically, that you can make a fair judgement.

That sounds like nonsense, but I believe it sincerely. If I stay somewhere for nothing I get away from whether or not it's good value – which is just as well, because that is an entirely subjective judgement that depends on your own income, outlook and experiences. What I can do is tell you what it feels like, and every time I've stayed in one of these places – without fail – after a few days I find myself longing to get away from the attitude and the atmosphere. It's a tangible sensation, a metaphysical version of the feeling you get over Christmas, when you've eaten far too many pigs in blankets, Quality Street and an entire year's worth of cheese. Of course the food is usually excellent in posh hotels, but that just means you eat too much and feel bloated while you're there. My own weakness is for a full English breakfast, but by the time you get to day three all you can face is a slim piece of melon and half a pack of Rennie.

All of this over-indulgence makes you feel very unattractive, which is then magnified a thousand fold by the staff and other clientele, who are usually beautiful and impeccably attired. Being in the presence of people who can afford to stay in these places means you also become utterly paranoid about your clothes, which are never the 'right' thing to wear. Uncomfortable or inappropriate clothing is disastrous for your digestion, too. The staff are usually totally over the top and constantly looking to be tipped, effectively asking you to pay them extra for being friendly: a strange idea that makes you uncomfortable whenever they do anything nice for you.

Rather oddly, the only other place I've stayed that conveyed an equally awful atmosphere, despite coming from an apparently polar-opposite perspective, was a Benedictine monastery. Anyone can stay there, as I did: one of the Rules of St Benedict is to offer free sanctuary to travellers. Perhaps that's not as enticing as a all-expenses-paid stay in a posh hotel, but stick with me. The monastery was comfortable but austere, with no luxuries of any kind, and you weren't allowed to speak when you were eating. This is more similar to a luxury hotel in attitude and tone than you might think. They both have an overwhelming feeling of oppression and uncertainty, because it's almost impossible to relax in either place. They are also both grounded in fear and very unfriendly (the monks were just as patronising as the hotel waiters), but one is free and the other costs £300–£500 a night. I suppose in one sense the hotels are better value – they entice you with promises of a break from normal life and rinse your credit card for the privilege, whereas monasteries tempt you in for nothing in the hope of securing your eternal soul.

Of course the biggest attraction of absurdly luxurious hotels lies in your brain rather than anything these places actually offer. The fact that I will never stay in the seven-star Burj Al Arab hotel in Dubai, for example (where every suite is on two floors and comes with a butler), allows me to imagine what it might be like to stay there, or more crucially to imagine the sort of person I would be *were* I ever able to afford to stay there.

Ocean Club Marbella appears to have been designed to make sure that people like me – who can't afford to go in even if they wanted to – can still see the pool and impeccably dressed waiters serving the absurdly young and attractive boys and girls their exclusive champagne. I was actually rather impressed by it in terms of the sheer vulgarity and superficiality it communicated. It was full of young women with luxurious hair and inflated bikinis, laughing animatedly next to bronzed men with stomachs of iron and designer stubble.

A little further up I found another beach club, slightly – but only very slightly – less obviously demanding to be stared at. It was called the Buddha Beach Bar and when I got home I found that its website proudly boasted the names of the footballers who had visited. I did recognise a footballer the day I was there and he stood out because he was the only one wearing clothes among a crowd of people in tiny swimming costumes. He looked a little odd in trousers, a shirt and a thin jumper, chatting to all these semi-naked people. But then I realised that this was how he revealed his status. The less 'right' you have to be there, the fewer clothes you must wear. Because he was a footballer – the Holy Grail of their clientele – he got to keep his clothes on.

Assuming the grave insult to the Buddhist faith was meant as a form of irony – I can't imagine Buddha putting up with the fawning conversation that took place between cocktails – it seemed much smaller than Ocean Club Marbella. But it did have a handy viewing point that you could lean on to gawp more comfortably at the people inside. It was like leaning on a gate and staring at a field of sheep. I had no sense of embarrassment gazing with my mouth open at the people inside both these beach clubs, reasoning that if people like me didn't stare at the people inside, the people being stared at wouldn't bother to come.

The inmates of the Buddha Beach Bar and Ocean Club Marbella left me wondering what the real purpose of a holiday is. Perhaps subconsciously we are all chasing this kind of experience – one that will make us feel like a celebrity or turn us, albeit briefly, into the rich and beautiful teenager all popular culture now seems to aspire to. We need something blissful to dream of while we're performing the often-mundane tasks that pay the mortgage and all the other monthly bills. The Buddha Beach Bar and Ocean Club Marbella offer a form of bliss that obviously works for some people – and let's be honest, we all have a version of it in our heads. We might not all dream of the shops, boats and beach bars of Puerto Banus, but we're all looking for something when we go away for our two weeks in the sun. Escape, oblivion, a few weeks to relax and read a book – aren't these all our version of the fantasy the luxury hotel resorts do their best to live up to? I've certainly been on holidays whose sole purpose was to envelop me in a kind of anaesthetic that would help me forget about my life and job back at home.

It's rarely a rewarding experience, though. Too often there is a chasm between the thoughts and expectations conjured from the pages of brochures about what our holidays will be like and the reality we find when we arrive. I once compiled a book of stories of holiday disasters to explore this idea. Chris Donald, the founder of *Viz*, wrote of his trip to an all-inclusive, five-star holiday resort in the Caribbean that cost him 'the price of a small house':

> I spent much of the time locked in our bathroom desperately trying to avoid the attention of the hotel staff. The bastards waited on you hand and foot. Every door was opened for you, dining chairs pulled out – and then pushed in once you'd lowered your arse...

The reality of the perfect holiday with an unlimited budget can still struggle to match up to the way you imagine it will be – even if you can afford it.

***

As my journey home on the Eurostar came to a close the following day, I began to jot down some notes for a talk on slow travel I was due to give later that day at the Larmer Tree Festival in Dorset. I had been invited to talk about how my fascination with the idea of travelling in a different way had resulted in a month-long journey with friends across England in a 1957 electric milk float back in 2007. That trip really was the definition of slow travel. We discovered on our first day (having done no planning whatsoever) that cooker sockets are the only power source in a domestic house capable of charging a vintage milk float. It was only then that we realised we would have to persuade a complete stranger to let us disconnect their cooker and wire our milk float directly into the mains of their house for eight hours, every day for a month, if we were to complete our planned journey.

It was interesting for me to revisit the themes and purpose of that trip in comparison with the beach bars of Marbella I'd just come from. The main difference between the two seemed, on the face of it, to be time. Most people don't have the time, or inclination perhaps, to spend a month driving across the country in a vintage milk float, but that shouldn't mean the philosophy behind the trip is unattainable. I knew it was possible to apply the ideas of slow travel to the snatches of time most people spend each year on their holidays, but why are so few people doing it? Why is everyone in such a rush?

This train of thought was confirmed a few hours later at the end of my talk. The festival was very much part of the slow philosophy and the audience seemed fascinated by our little expedition. I pointed out that, when you read great travel books, you find that most of the writers are slow travellers; they've just never been pulled together under that collective umbrella. As I was packing away a lady came up and said to me, 'I love reading travel books and you're right, the best ones are about slow travel, but those books are travelogues. They're another kind of escape. They don't help *me* to travel differently.'

She was right, of course. It's one thing for the Paul Therouxs, Bruce Chatwins and Jonathan Rabans of this world to spend months and months travelling slowly around the world, but what about the rest of us with jobs and families? So that became the purpose of this book. To define what it means to be a slow, or idle, traveller and find out how to change the way we think about travel in the small amount of time we spend away from work.

Chapter 2

Stay at home

Home is so sad. It stays as it was left,
Shaped to the comfort of the last to go
As if to win them back...
Philip Larkin, 'Home Is So Sad'

Reading these lines made me wonder whether this notion of home could be extended beyond the bricks and mortar of my house and out into the countryside around it as well. Was the landscape where I live – largely unthinkingly – also sad at my neglect? In my love of travel, had I begun to view my home as a means to an end, a destination I occupy but don't really understand? Did it seek to win me back? Wherever you happen to be geographically, travel actually takes place in your brain, so applying the mindset of the traveller to where you live is an interesting way to think about what it means to go on holiday.

On a bright day in November, I headed out with a rucksack on my back to explore some of the places under my nose that I usually drive though at great speed. I was determined to answer Larkin in my own way and to treat my home with the same spirit of adventure that inspired one of my favourite travel writers, Laurie Lee. Walking out of his front door with the perspective of a traveller, rather than a trapped teenager, altered the way he saw and felt about the landscape of his childhood.

Reading the opening pages of *As I Walked Out One Midsummer Morning* again some 20 years after discovering the book for the first time at school was like the feeling of weightlessness you get when you step into a hammock. It transpires that the voice in my ear throughout my life, whispering of the enchantment of slow travel, has always been Lee. The words of the first chapter re-formed themselves like welcoming hugs from long-cherished friends in a pub on a summer's night.

In 1930, at the age of 19, Laurie Lee left his home in the Cotswolds on foot with a tent, a violin, a change of clothes, a tin of treacle biscuits and some cheese. He walked down to Southampton to see the sea for the first time, before heading to London, where he worked for a year as a labourer. Then he began his travels in Spain. Penning his memoir with 30 years' hindsight, he recalls leaving home on the first day of his trip:

> I was lucky, I know, to have been setting out at that time, in a landscape not yet bulldozed for speed. Many of the country roads still followed their original tracks, drawn by packhorse or lumbering cartwheel, hugging the curve of a valley or yielding to a

promontory like the wandering line of a stream. It was not, after all, so very long ago, but no one could make that journey today. Most of the old roads have gone, and the motor car, since then, has begun to cut the landscape to pieces, through which the hunched-up traveller races at gutter height, seeing less than a dog in a ditch.

Of course the world has been forced to concede even more ground in the search for greater speed and efficiency today. In Southampton, Lee builds up enough courage to start busking with his violin and soon manages to scrape up enough money to keep him on the move and away from the clutches of a regular job. I then read with a chuckle that he stopped briefly in Chichester on his journey along the coast, but this is noted only because within moments of his starting to play 'Bless This House' in front of the cathedral the police move him on. I'm sure exactly the same thing would happen today.

It's not just Lee who sees travel as being inextricably linked to taking your time. Over the years I've found most travel writers revel in it. For example, Paul Theroux on the misery of air travel in *The Old Patagonian Express*: 'You define a good flight by negatives: you didn't get hijacked, you didn't crash, you didn't throw up, you weren't late, you weren't nauseated by the food. So you are grateful.' In *Ghost Train to the Eastern Star* Theroux even describes himself as 'an idle traveller'. In *What Am I Doing Here?* Bruce Chatwin is clear that the speed at which you travel defines the experience: 'Walking is a virtue, tourism is a deadly sin.' Patrick Leigh Fermor, who went on an epic walk through Eastern Europe in his late teens, writes in *A Time of Gifts:* 'All horsepower corrupts'. And there are plenty more we'll come to later.

A few hundred years ago there was no option but to travel slowly along the contours and channels of the earth and sea; indeed that was the very definition of travel. The effort required in those days meant that those who did go on long journeys came back as heroes, viewed by their home-locked peers as superior women and men.

In 1749 Thomas Nugent, who wrote a guidebook of destinations one might seek on a Grand Tour (more on this later), describes travel as 'the only means of improving the understanding, and of acquiring a high degree of reputation'. He goes on, 'The first civilised nations...honoured even such as made but short voyages...the title of philosophers and conquerors.' He traces the lineage of those who head abroad to seek knowledge, whom he describes as sages, back to the Argonauts and Odysseus in Homer's *Odyssey*. I'm not sure anyone would draw such grandiose comparisons with the average holidaymaker today.

Lee's adventure starts with him walking out of his front door and off into the unknown. While most of us, including me, would find that practically impossible to do – what with jobs, families and responsibilities to come back to – we could all surely still manage to live within that mindset for a single day. I wondered whether it would be possible to experience a hint of what Lee writes about so movingly on a day's walk from my own front door.

I have made one particular journey between Chichester and the village of South Harting on the other side of the South Downs regularly in a car since I was six years old. I have watched the landscape of that route remain largely unchanged for 30 years. Crossing the Downs at night terrified me as a small child, and I always relaxed when we came through to the other side. As I got older this sense of wildness became profoundly captivating, but I'd never actually explored the route on foot in all the years I've been visiting and now living here. I had never got lost in the landscape in between. So that was my plan. I was excited and slightly cross with myself for never having got round to doing something so obvious before.

***

It took me 25 minutes to escape the city, via a newsagent where I filled my bag with junk food to stave off later physical collapse. The main road I drive along most days to take Wilf to school had few idiosyncrasies for a pedestrian to find, save for the summer carrier bags shoved in the beech hedges by schoolchildren, now revealed as the hedges dropped their withered leaves. The sun was low and behind me, and would be my only companion for the day. Ducking down at a bridge, I found the converted railway line tarmacked as far north as the village of West Dean. The old cutting shielded me from the housing estates that have appeared in the last 50 years. I paused for a while trying to catch leaves as they fell, to ensure good luck for the journey ahead. Despite pirouetting in embarrassment in front of a series of joggers and mums with prams, I couldn't catch one. Much further down the path, once I was no longer trying, I held out my hand and one landed in my outstretched palm, which seemed a fitting omen.

Autumn should by now have been giving way to winter, but the squirrels looked vaguely bemused by the unseasonably warm air as they bounced along the wide path of fallen leaves. Poison pie and lawyer's wig mushrooms poked out of the squishy crevices between the tarmac and the oak litter. Eventually the path led me out of the cutting and the sun warmed my shoulders again. I could see the South Downs on the horizon, beneath distant clouds the colour of white dishcloths that have been left in the sink too long. The Downs looked bewilderingly far away. They were my Misty Mountains, Moomin Valley and Hundred Acre Wood all rolled into one. Concerned at my complete ignorance when it comes to estimating any distance with my own eyes, I stopped and measured the route on my map with a curling forefinger. Twelve miles should be easy enough.

A mixed perfume of yellow-flowered gorse and browning ferns kept me company as I pottered to a hump that carried a road above me. Only once I'd gone under it did I realise that it was a bridge I must have driven over a thousand times, with my father sounding the horn to see if anyone was coming the other way. For all those years the path I had just walked out of the city centre had been completely unknown to me.

Ten minutes later I climbed a bank and left the path of the old railway line, joining the main road through the village of Lavant. The seasonal river of the same name meandered below for a while, but then tumbled away down into a meadow. To my right I spotted a viewpoint called the Trundle that I had recently taken the time to visit, largely on account of local assurances that this was the spot that inspired William Blake to write so powerfully of the English countryside in his song 'Jerusalem'. I had previously spent a few hours in the local second-hand bookshop to see if I could find any evidence for this and a few other rather grand claims about my immediate vicinity. No one can be completely sure whether that view evoked the words 'green and pleasant land', but Blake did spend a few years living in Felpham on the coast near Bognor Regis and was known to ride to Lavant to visit friends on a weekly basis. He would also have been able to see the Downs from his bedroom window. You can be sure of this because from the top of the Trundle you can see an unmistakable white building that looks like a series of strange white tents down by the sea. That white building is the Butlin's holiday camp that has since been built within earshot of where Blake used to live.

I left 'Jerusalem' and stayed with the A286, intending to do so for only a little way. I was trying to find the route of the old Roman road that would take me to the South Downs Way on the other side of the woods on the climbing horizon. It was marked clearly on my map as emerging in a typically straight line from behind a house on the road. The B road to South Harting dived down into a valley to my left as I plodded on up the hill. In the scream of the passing articulated lorries my high spirits began to morph into questioning voices. The familiar landscape had grown in size because of my languid progress and my brain was struggling to update the default setting it usually assumed when it interpreted this particular scenery – most often through the window of a speeding car. It had taken me an hour to travel a distance that usually took me less than 10 minutes, and the road and exhaust fumes, mixed with my neurological confusion, threatened to consume my blind optimism.

After navigating the pot-holed verge and thundering lorries, I finally found the house I was looking for, but there was no sign of a path behind it. I could see hedges and fences zigzagging over the route of where it should have been in the fields up ahead. This was rather dispiriting news. Without that path there was no obvious way to connect where I was standing and where I needed to go.

After more fruitless searching, I found a gate that was slightly open leading around the perimeter wall of a large house. Forlornly I hoped it would take me to a field further up where the path, surely, would be. I walked nervously, eyeing the windows of the manor, but I don't think anyone saw me. Eventually I dived into the safety of a copse of beech and holly trees.

The ground was tinder dry. I looked at my watch but could tell I was no longer entirely contained by it. Then I realised that 'it' had happened. Back on the road I had crossed some kind of portal and my frame of mind and perspective had changed. It felt as though I'd been walking much longer – or much more deeply, perhaps – than the number of seconds and minutes my watch indicated. As I entered that isolated copse of trees, walking on the dry, rusting earth, I knew I was truly on my way.

Back in the 19th century Henry David Thoreau wrote in the conclusion to *Walden* (his treatise on the succour to be found in a simple rural life away from the world of busy men): 'If a man does not keep pace with his companions, perhaps it is because he hears a different drummer. Let him step to the music which he hears, however measured or far away.' Such noble and wise words are tempered slightly when you discover his rural idyll relied on his mum performing many of his mundane household duties, but I do think it is this impulse to slow down that all travellers share. But rather than each hearing a different kind of music, as Thoreau suggests, I wonder if these people are living with an alternative concept of time in mind. The thrill of living in the moment, which is the real destination of all journeys, is what the greatest travel writers are revealing in their meticulous descriptions of the places they go and the people they meet.

On Lee's journey across the Downs 80 years ago he encountered people living within a different concept of time. He made his way north from Worthing and came across a line of professional tramps, all of whom lived on the road, on the latest leg of their annual circuit of the country. They were a kind of 1930s-style hunter-gatherer tribe and one of them soon took pity on the undernourished Lee, calling him a 'poor little bleeder':

> He was a tramp to his bones, always wrapping and unwrapping himself, and picking over his bits and pieces. He wasn't looking for work; this was simply his life, and he carefully rationed his energies – never passing a patch of grass that looked good for a shakedown, nor a cottage that seemed ripe for charity. He said his name was Alf, but one couldn't be sure, as he called me Alf, and everyone else.

The tramps' nomadic lives were seasonal, touring the countryside through the spring and summer, often heading between local agricultural fairs and taking refuge in cities as winter approached. Lee describes Alf as slow but not lazy, living according to his own rhythm of time rather than the one imposed on everyone else.

***

There is no doubt in my mind, despite an otherwise solid faith in the rules and methods of science, that our brains are capable of experiencing different kinds of time. We all know time can 'speed up' when we're doing something we've been desperately looking forward to or 'slow down' when we have to do something we dread. Weekends go much more quickly than the first two days of the week in the mind of anyone with a full-time job. You have to be careful when talking about time, however. Few rational people would dare claim today that there is any kind of real time other than the trajectory of past, present and future.

But the idea that slow travel accessed a different way of experiencing time, and that travel writing itself perhaps originated with Homer's *Odyssey*, was encouraging. A few years ago I read that the Greeks had two gods of time. The first, Chronos, we know all about. He is the god of chronological, measurable, equal, scientific time. One second after another, perhaps forever. We all wear watches in honour of him. Chronos doesn't represent the kind of travel Laurie Lee wrote about or that 'Alf' lived within, or my slow travel experiences, but his sort of time is surely what we experience most of our working lives and indeed most of our holidays too. Holidays offer solace from the clock-watching day-to-day routine we all need a break from, but we are imprisoned by them too. By his very nature Chronos makes us look back and ahead rather than concentrating on the here and now. He is the enemy when a holiday lies too far ahead, when we are actually there (because it goes too fast) and when we get home afterwards (as he propels us away into the future). All we have left are the holiday snaps that don't quite capture how we felt at the time.

Interestingly, though, for the idle traveller there is another Greek god of time – one I would argue is more in keeping with the experience of slow travel – but his name is unknown to most of us. He is called Kairos and he is the god of what is known as divine time, those moments in life when you have to act with courage or lament your inaction forever. In the few images you can find of him on the internet he looks rather odd. He has winged feet – because he's so fast – and a big quiff of hair on his forehead, but the rest of his head is shaved completely bald. When you see him coming you have to grab hold of his hair to stop him and embrace the fleeting opportunity he brings. If, on the other hand, you dither and don't act, once he has passed by there is nothing to grab hold of and the moment is lost forever. Kairos is not about linear time. You'll find him in the eternal present and haunting your memories of missed opportunities. We've all experienced Kairos. We all know that feeling, or rather that kind of time. Kairos inspired the famous maxim *carpe diem* (seize the day). He marks the choices we make or don't make that map our lives into the journeys they become. These are the actions we make in the moment, the ones that change our loves and lives forever. But in the world of haste that we're all usually confined within, Kairos simply doesn't exist at all.

***

On the other side of the island of trees – that was no more than 20 strides wide – I ate some sandwiches I'd brought from home and began to feel delightfully foolish. The Roman road clearly no longer existed, not even in the memory of the landscape in the way old drovers' paths sometimes do. I was doing something that a week ago would have seemed quite mad, but I was drenched in contentment. I knew it was an ephemeral feeling, I had work to deal with tomorrow, but sitting there I felt quite free. Time was not rushing away from me.

The non-existent road used to be a major route connecting Chichester to the Roman city of Calleva Atrebatum, which perhaps fittingly no longer exists either. In *I Saw Two Englands*, written less than a decade after Lee made his journey, author and traveller H V Morton describes a visit to the empty fields that lie between modern-day Reading and Basingstoke. He ponders how a city that stood for 400 years as part of the Roman Empire could have been so utterly consumed by nature while others, notably Chichester, were reused and rebuilt. No one knows the answer to this conundrum even today, but it put the concept of 'owning' land into focus. I loved the idea that for hundreds of years the town just fell into decay, the people who lived nearby content to let it drift because in those days it was quite normal for large sections of the landscape to be uncatalogued and untamed. In that wildness the landscape would reclaim its own kind of geographical imagination, expressing itself through nerve-jangling stories shared around communal fires that we have no way of conjuring today.

The lack of path meant that I was now stranded and trespassing, so I was on an illegal adventure rather than a sanctioned walk. The map I'd invested such high hopes in wasn't much help. I could see the steep climb of the Downs and the woods I was heading for, but plotting a direct course between there and myself was legally impossible. I had become a boat marooned by perilous rocks of private land hidden beneath the sea.

At that point an emperor butterfly flew past, clearly as confused by the warmth as the squirrels, and then a buzzard wheeled overhead – so low he obviously hadn't noticed me beneath the trees. This was more evidence that my perceptions were changing. Blending into your surroundings to the point that wildlife doesn't notice you is always a comforting sign. I was now travelling at the pace required to acknowledge that the countryside itself was not a backdrop, but vitally alive. The butterfly came back for a second look and landed by my feet while the cars of people with 'important things to do' charged defiantly along the road down below. The same road I'd travelled so many times before in a car. The thought of relying on it so often now felt oddly desperate and functional. I finished my lunch, collected my rubbish and set off purposefully in a straight line where the ancient road should have been. Path or no path, I had decided to raise the centreboard on my little dinghy and take my chances with the sea.

The sun projected my shadow in the direction of the Downs and I settled on that as a bearing. As I walked, very respectfully and carefully, the notion of a footpath, or rather lack of one, began to bother me far more than the hedges and fences that blocked my way. If you drafted a map of the country and only coloured in the parts you are allowed to walk on, I wager the nation would look a very spindly and monochrome place. It's all very well having these beautiful vistas but it's a pedestrian safari, fenced in by imaginary walls that let us stare at the countryside but not to feel or smell its abundant complexity. I began to imagine metaphorical monkeys bending my ears as I veered away from the legal pathway. I wondered whether it limits our imagination to be prevented from enjoying the land in this way. Only the pheasants seem to have genuine freedom to roam the countryside, but one day having to have your head blown off in return is quite a high price to pay.

An hour or so later I emerged onto a legal path, slightly blooded from barbed wire and sweating profusely. I had been hopelessly lost but was now on track, in a manner of speaking. My shadow had failed me somewhere among a field of decaying sunflowers and I had to trudge along the main road for half a mile before turning right behind a farm. I climbed the country lane and breathed more easily, reasoning that the risk of being shot by an irate farmer had now surely diminished. I had heard whisperings for months that red kites were nesting in the South Downs and some had been seen as far south as Chichester. I hadn't seen any myself, apart from a few possible blurred sightings from the car, but now, almost as soon as I got off the road, I thought I spotted one far above in a thermal. I was confident of the shape and flight style but couldn't be completely certain. Then the road dipped down and off almost in a right angle and suddenly at head height I saw the unmistakable scarecrow arms of two red kites hanging nonchalantly. It was a moment of pure joy for a bird-of-prey fan like me. Kites are reclaiming the British countryside and it's a wonderful thing to see.

As I came to the edge of the woods I looked back for a sign of the Roman road, but any trace of it is long gone. A few weeks later I learned that had I been around in Roman times I wouldn't have been allowed to use it anyway. Roads were kept clear for merchants and the army; peasants like me would have relied on our own routes that crossed between villages and were far more higgledy-piggledy. The land was wooded, farmed hills and fields alternating between those left to recover from the summer and those full of the lush early leaves of winter vegetables. The range of browns, oranges and greens assaulting my vision combined with the now sinking sun gave the sky a white-purple hue.

I longed for the woods and began bounding in anticipation as they approached. Walking alone and lost in woodland is one of my favourite daydreams, but it wasn't to be. The West Dean Forest has a few public bridleways, but the paths that lead most tantalisingly into the deep all have signs that shout PRIVATE! NO PUBLIC RIGHT OF WAY. Rather than dive into the depths of the forest I would have to paddle around the edge instead. Again I spotted the pheasants roaming freely and sulked momentarily. Still, a diversion would mean slower progress, so I embraced the inconvenience. I also began to hear the sounds of trees being felled inside. It was obviously a working forest and no doubt a litigious walker who got a nasty splinter justified the rest of us being kept away.

Walking the edges of the pine forest took the sun away from me for the first time since I had seen the Downs. Seemingly abandoned machinery and vast piles of felled trees under tight tarpaulin produced a sense of contented loneliness as the sodden path beneath my feet began to give way. Eventually a path appeared that I was allowed to walk along; it led into a dark cave of pine branches, coloured by the brown tendrils of decaying fern. The floor of the forest had been deadened through management and lack of sunlight, allowing a fern-like moss the colour of AstroTurf to swarm over the litter, giving it a lurid fake beauty like some strange life form found at the bottom of the sea. The contrast between the lines of trees in the shadowy darkness and the bright green forest floor was bewitching.

According to my map I had nearly arrived at the spine of the South Downs Way, from where I would head west towards the mighty Harting Hill, a local viewpoint that again I had never seen. The path became a bridleway and soon I saw the familiar sight of a brown, unassuming 'footpath' sign. It pointed in three directions: one up towards the South Downs Way, another back from where I had come and the last down into the forest behind me. A fellow walker passing the other way paused as I dithered. A strange mirroring of responses followed as we looked at each other, wondering if we were too close and would have to acknowledge each other, or if we were safe and far enough away. He was the only other walker I'd seen so far that day but I was lost in my own thoughts and in no mood for polite conversation. I turned and he walked off. The new path headed in the direction of the word 'ruin' I'd just noticed on the map. I was a long way from home now, alone in woodland having made it as far as the ridge of the Downs, but in this moment of relative triumph a fierce doubt began to niggle me.

I knew the trees to my left were predominantly pine, and beyond the pathway that skirted around the edge of the wood I'd spotted occasional beech trees, but beyond those I realised I was struggling to interpret my surroundings. I glimpsed many birds and heard many songs and calls as the wood thickened, but to my shame I cannot tell you what species they were or what those songs mean. Nor can I relate in the style of the great nature writers like Roger Deakin or Chris Yates the detailed seasonal changes taking place around me. As I yomped back into the woods towards the ruin, I realised the countryside was a language filled with concepts that were hidden from me. I knew so little about the individual parts that made it up.

The passionate and learned prose that experts use to commune with their environment always inspires me, but leaves me feeling slightly in awe as well. Is our casual observation of landscape as meaningful as it could be? Can we really appreciate it if we are ignorant of the birds, trees, grasses, wild flowers and animals that combine to create it? Learning about the nature around us is, of course, something few of us have the time to do and I felt overwhelmed because my knowledge was so patchy. I began compulsively to take photographs of everything so I could fake it and check them all later with a Google image search before describing them to you in detail, but the truth of my ignorance is much more interesting. Happily Deakin came to my rescue later that night, writing sternly in *Notes from Walnut*

Tree Farm: 'There's a myth in this country that the professionals are better at things than the amateurs: that they know more, and get things right. I believe the opposite to be true.'

He was talking of politicians rather than brain surgeons, of course, but the sentiment applied just as well to me. The point of these great interpreters of the landscape is to inspire us to make discoveries of our own, not for their writings to be used as a substitute. As I walked deeper into the forest in search of the ruin a related memory made me laugh out loud, breaking the silence of the woods for a moment. After years of being baffled by Morrissey's patronising tone in The Smiths song 'Ask' – 'Nature is a language, can't you read?' – I now realised exactly what he meant.

The ruin was a phantom, either so comprehensively overgrown that it no longer existed or pulled down without the gods of Ordnance Survey being informed. I emerged from a hedge and saw two mountain bikers riding along what must have been a path. The path. The South Downs Way. When I reached it the horizon fell away to my right and I could see a hill climbing towards Arundel, but the rising path obscured the view to my left ahead of me. I stomped hungrily, desperate to see the vista I'd worked so hard for. Soon the land dropped down, the sun marking the undulations of the field with tufted silhouettes. The banks of the Downs became almost sheer in places and the headland of Harting Hill came into sight beyond another hill crowded with pine trees. Now that I was on the ridge, with each step forward the landscape began to unfold a little more until the flatlands of Hampshire emerged beneath me. I could see for miles down across a plateau I had driven through countless times without knowing anything of the land; those trenches of convenient tarmac had always sped me through it. I began to smile the smile of a man who has glimpsed the extent of his own ignorance, but who is inspired to learn more rather than be crushed by it. I stood there for some time smiling, my deep breaths floating off into the view like cobwebs, spiralling adrift in the breeze.

***

It's not just nature we struggle to understand without the terms and names needed to define it. The same is true of human experience itself. If your language doesn't have a word for an idea, your brain will find it difficult to retain it. That may sound like a small problem, not having a word for a concept, but it's your language, just as much as the rules of the universe, that determine how you think and approach your life. For most people Kairos will be an example of this. As soon as you learn of the existence of moments that have the capacity to change your life forever and have a word to contain those possibilities, it feels as though you've intuitively understood the concept your entire life, you just couldn't verbalise it until now.

There are many other concepts like this – I'm a detective of these words myself – and I came across a fascinating one while writing this book. It is the Hebrew word *tzedakah*. There is no direct translation of this word into English. It means charity, but it also means justice. In English, charity means giving to those in need, and justice means getting what you deserve. Those are two very different concepts for anyone whose native tongue is English. There's a potential chasm of political argument between the two because while you may give charity to someone, combining it with justice assumes they are entitled to the gift in the first place, which in turn means it's not an act of charity after all. Each definition is a parallel line that the word *tzedakah* manages to connect. It's the language you think in rather than the concept itself that enforces those parallel lines. *Tzedakah* seems a perfectly reasonable concept when you have a word that expresses it.

None of this is a problem for speakers of Hebrew, for whom the act of charitable giving is by definition also a question of justice. There's no debate in their minds between the two concepts, it just is. Forming that idea in your head using a language that can't classify it into a single word is *very* difficult, even if you feel you can grab the idea. It's arguable whether or not someone who speaks only English could ever imagine that concept on their own.

I'll give you another example that relates to time. In the Arctic the Inuit have a word *invatarru* that means the future. But it also means the past, because in their culture time is cyclical. That kind of time cannot have an empty void to dread at the end of your life, nor the need for a myth of eternal life when you die. Regardless of whether or not the idea happens to be 'true', it's very tricky to comprehend the vastness of the concept and how it would alter the way we lived our lives if that was how we thought about time.

What it does prove is that the impact of language on how we experience the world is much more far reaching than we might think. It puts us at the mercy of the ideas our language is able to explain. This is why the death of any language is such a profound loss to us all, because when a language dies so too do any concepts it contains that our language does not. The result of that is, quite literally, unimaginable. The thing we have to thank for the spread of these concepts that enrich all our lives and make us see the world and the way we live in life-enhancing ways is, of course, travel.

As I began to see the extent of the countryside I had not experienced despite it being under my nose all the time, I realised the same must be true of all kinds of concepts. Imagine all the ideas and ways of looking at the world that our brains could understand intuitively but that we are closed to because our own language is too restrictive. The language that we use to interpret our very consciousness becomes like a road that funnels us through the landscape surrounding our homes. On the one hand it offers us a trusted and predictable route through our conscious experience of the world, but on the other denies us new ways of enjoying our local landscape, and the limitless other ways of thinking and experiencing life. The idle traveller has time to notice and reflect on this, of course, because he or she avoids the well-trodden path – the obvious ideas and concepts – while those in a rush to consume the world are trammelled by familiarity and convenience.

***

I passed lots of other walkers along the next stretch of the path and saw within five minutes more people than I'd so far seen all day. Most of them were snacking on the countryside, scaling the hill from their cars with flitting children and dogs yapping around them, but every now and then I'd spot a fellow traveller gorging themselves on their surroundings, like me. One man in blue Lycra limped along with a grizzled face, walking on the outside edges of each foot like a demented Chaplin impersonator. His map whipped around his bottom in a polythene flap as he winced along, no doubt from blisters, offering me a polite and whispered 'Hello there' in response to my staring at him for too long.

I had sunglasses on now and felt like an embattled conqueror. I had eaten most of the food and finished off most of the water I had brought, so my bag was light and I sprang across the grassy track to avoid schlepping into holes of mud. Home seemed a very long way away indeed. The wind began to remind the afternoon that it was November, but an extra jumper kept me warm. Then the woods consumed my path and the view was gone.

Hemmed in on the one hand by woods I was prohibited from entering and by private land on the other, the path funnelled me up and down and round a hill like a swimming-pool flume. Eventually it spat me out in front of a vast grassy mound, and despite emerging blisters of my own and the sun beginning to pull away and overtake me, I had to stop and scale it. The barrow was one of many Bronze Age burial mounds across the country constructed to line up with sunset on Midsummer's Day and I'd had no idea it existed. The first was by no means the largest, and I ended up climbing all five until I settled on the biggest of them.

Estimated to be between 3,000 and 4,000 years old, these barrows are our pyramids, built around the same time as Stonehenge. British schoolchildren know more about the burial rituals of Egyptian pharaohs than they do about our own ancient lords and kings, but ours sit here silently, marked only by a weathered and well-meaning, rather tattered sign, unassumingly ignored for only the intrepid to stumble upon. Sheep and cattle graze freely as a way to manage the land. You can't imagine animals being left to roam many of the world's 4,000-year-old human monuments, but in this case it's rather appropriate. The barrows give us a sign that our ancestors had begun to make permanent marks on the landscape and embrace farming in a way that would have been unthinkable to their nomadic forefathers.

Anthropologists think that human beings became 'like us' in terms of the cultural emergence of behaviours such as religion, cooking, games and language around 50,000 years ago, but travelling had been part of our lives hundreds of thousands of years before then. *Homo sapiens* (Latin for 'knowing man') continued to be a travelling people, living as hunter-gatherers. This life of constant movement took them out of Africa and across into the world, crossing the bridge of land that until around 8,500 years ago connected modern Britain with mainland Europe. It was only after the agricultural Neolithic Revolution between 8,000 and 3,000 BC that they, or perhaps we, began to live in settlements we would recognise as early villages and towns. It's worth remembering that of those hundreds of millennia it's only in the last ten that 'our' lives have become based in a single place. It's surely no surprise then that the echo of this life on the road, the free, wandering spirits of men and women remembered in our very DNA, should inspire the concept of travel so profoundly in us today. Or that being on the move – when we embrace what that really means – allows our brains to revel in a way of thinking that feels strange yet reassuringly familiar at the same time.

* * *

As an aside for those of a naturally idle disposition like me, recent studies have found that the average hunter-gatherer worked only around three days a week. Hunting and foraging for food were much more efficient than the daily grind of agricultural toil that would replace them, allowing more leisure time than most of us experience today. For one thing, hunter-gatherer parents were much more hands-on than we are. Of course, with the advent of agriculture people began to grow more food than they needed for themselves and had to work longer hours in order to protect and nurture it. This put them at risk of famine if they had a bad harvest but gave them the possibility of a surplus if it was a good one. From that we can begin to see the path that took us from 'knowing man' into 'capitalist man', with a life swinging between the boom and bust of the modern global economy.

***

I climbed down from the barrow and rejoined the path, my sense of adventure beginning to fail as every other step inflated a blister, bringing a *thsss* sound out of my mouth. My feelings echoed Laurie Lee's after the initial euphoria of the first few hours of his adventure: 'That first day alone – and now I was really alone at last – steadily declined in excitement and vigour...As I walked I was taunted by echoes of home.' But I steeled myself and trudged on as the sun began to slip away. The path ducked and weaved around the edges of a deep bowl with a stone farmhouse squatting in its centre, as though it had been built at the base of a reclaimed quarry. The rich colours of earlier in the day were now fixed in a dusky grey and I passed a small memorial to a fighter pilot whose plane had crashed here during the Battle of Britain.

Painfully the path fell down and down, but I could see that further on I would have to reclaim this lost height and a fair bit more besides on yet another hill before the might of Harting. Bizarrely, an entire rugby team then jogged up the hill towards me, each man snorting and spitting, focusing on his own run. As I came to the side of the farmhouse the pathway hugged the edges of vast chalk mounds, which a couple of walkers had chosen to scale to watch the setting sun. I weaved down and round and then began to climb again, resting my hands on my thighs as I trudged up, my breath escaping before most of it had the chance to reach the bronchi of my lungs.

When I finally made it to the top of Harting Hill I collapsed on my back, momentarily defeated. The view of the village I had been heading towards all day, South Harting, with the green spire of the church beneath me and the smoke churning from the chimneys of some of the village houses, restored me – but not for long. On the plus side, my attention was briefly grabbed by a small building I could see on the top of another hill to my left. It was a folly – one of hundreds of literally pointless buildings you'll find in the English countryside, often put up in the 17th or 18th century in the aftermath of a rich aristocrat returning from the Grand Tour. This one is called the Vandalian Tower and was erected to celebrate the 21st birthday of Sir Harry Fetherstonhaugh, the future Lady Hamilton's first illicit conquest. The tower became a house of ill repute from where sozzled revellers were placed in wheelbarrows and pushed home by the nonplussed servants of nearby Uppark (where H G Wells' mother worked as a housekeeper and the author himself lived as a child). Now only half of the folly remains, in a fenced-off island surrounded by fields of corn.

I walked faster, sensing the end, and bounded down the hill, ignoring the wincing pain of my feet, chasing the prize of a pint of local ale. As darkness began to block the last fragments of light that glinted through the trees I finally reached the road – that shoelace connecting the village with the city I called home; the tightrope that until that day had confined my imagination the hundreds of times I'd travelled along it between where I was going and where I had been. I was ashamed of what I now knew existed but had never made the time to see. I stopped for a while to slow the frantic beating of my heart.

A road. For so long in my mind it had been an unquestioned symbol of travel, adventure and escape, but in reality it's a lousy metaphor. A road is a tunnel that traps you in linear places, linear concepts and linear time. It provides ease and convenience, but cheats you of everything you might learn if you only had the time and curiosity to leave it.

My final steps took me into the town and I was now yearning for a pub with a roaring fire and a hearty landlady. I felt I deserved it. There was no street lighting, so it was perilous in the extreme walking on the main road in what was now total darkness. The pub I'd most wanted to visit was closed, but there was another further up the road and I could see it was open. I pushed the door. The air inside was damp and cold; two television sets grunted out the football results and as I walked in six middle-aged men stared at me. The landlord summoned the effort to raise his eyebrows as a means of saying hello. I couldn't face being in there among them, so I mumbled something and left. And then it began to rain.

Lee's first night ended equally miserably, all his hopes and excitement culminating in a night asleep under the stars in a field. He woke at midnight in the pouring rain being nibbled by beetles and, most frighteningly, dribbled on by a cow. It was here that I parted from his delightful company, glad that I had joined him for only a single day. Shivering now in the November rain, I made a phone call. Half an hour later my loves arrived, with cries of 'Daddy!'

***

When we got home I put my feet up, ordered an Indian takeaway and drank a bottle of beer. The beauty of treating your own home with a sense of adventure is the local knowledge you don't normally have time to acquire. That day I had gone north. I unfolded my map and read the names of places I'd seen on signs but had never made the time to visit before. My eyes had become accustomed to ignoring what was under my nose, but now I was beginning to see my home with the mindset of a traveller and I wouldn't neglect it any more.

Chapter 3

Be your own guide

I know but one freedom, and that is the freedom of the mind
Antoine de Saint-Exupery

When you start to plan a trip abroad your first impulse is often to reach for a traditional guidebook. You go into a bookshop and seek out the travel section. There the world is divided and subdivided into blocks of information. You go to the section relevant to you, find the country you're looking for and make a decision between the various branded guides. You choose a brand you trust or that has been successfully marketed to you and then you have a portable reference tool. Simple. Now you can relax, knowing you have what you need to make the most of your trip, because you wouldn't want to make anything less than the most of it, now would you?

If you're really excited you'll start reading the book as soon as you get home, perhaps marking key sections or 'must sees' with yellow post-it notes. Or, if you're anything like the way I used to be, you'll forget about it completely until the morning you leave. On the journey you'll start to read it guiltily, as though it's a kind of homework you've not got around to. You'll probably skip the history section because it's a bit boring and find yourself reading 'how to get there', which you don't need because you're already on your way. Then you come to the 'where to stay' section and get a pang of terror in case the place you have chosen features prominently in where *not* to stay. After that you feel irritated because where you are staying is not mentioned at all, or it's more expensive than everywhere else and you feel rubbish for being so badly prepared.

Now in a suitable state of anxiety you start on the safety information, where to find your embassy, how not to offend the locals, that kind of thing. You read it diligently at first but then get bored because, let's face it, if something goes that wrong it will probably mean your bag with the guidebook inside has been pinched, so it will be useless anyway.

Next you come to the list of places anyone visiting 'has to see', because not to see them would mark you out as a travel failure. If you're very lucky this section will be juxtaposed with a part about where to find the 'real' version of your destination, a tacit acknowledgement that the previous sites are unreal, characterisations of something that used to be.

By this stage you're probably thinking this doesn't feel much like a holiday, what with all these pitfalls and suggested itineraries filling up the short number of days you have to relax. In fact you begin to realise that this book is marinating your brain in guilt. It's full of boxes for you to tick and to-do lists that you already know you won't get around to. Finally, you'll find the one page you think you might actually use, which is the map, but because it's entombed in all this panicky information – and you'll get a much bigger, colourful and free one in the lobby of your hotel the second you arrive – you won't make use of it either.

I'm being a little unfair here: these guidebooks are often written and published by people who are passionate about the destination and are only trying to help. They are also written to a specification that probably doesn't give the authors the freedom to do exactly what they want to do, so lists and 'blockbuster' sights end up taking priority. My main problem with these books is that they set your brain on a narrow path through your travel experience – a path that leaves very little for *you* to do. I remember talking to a friend who had been to Rome numerous times. As her latest trip approached she said something very interesting over a glass of wine. 'I'm really looking forward to it because I've been there so many times I've already seen the things you "have to see", so now I can just go and enjoy myself. This time there's no pressure to actually *do* anything.' Eureka!

My advice would be to go back to that bookshop and look again at the way these well-meaning books demystify and de-personalise your trip before you've even thought about what you want to do. The clue is in the name. If you look up the word 'guide' in the dictionary you'll find that it means 'a person who leads or shows the way' or 'a person who conducts travellers or tours'. Now, unless you're heading off to trek the length of the Amazon or to climb the North Face of the Eiger, do you really want to be led or conducted? By using a guidebook you're acknowledging that you need this help in the first place, slotting yourself into the pigeonhole for the nervous traveller. But there's no need to be nervous: everywhere I've ever been was full of really nice, kind people who were very happy to help if I needed it.

Guidebooks weren't always like this, however. In 1829 Karl Baedeker published his first travel guide – to the Rhine in Germany – and the Baedeker series became the benchmark that all subsequent guidebooks would fail in comparison to. Karl's son Fritz was at the helm by the time the railways had conquered the world, and introduced a series of automobile guides soon after Karl Benz built his first car. Baedeker was the first person to use the star grading system for hotels, but it was the attention to detail and encyclopaedic knowledge of the destination that gave his books such a wide appeal.

At the time of writing, a copy of the *Baedeker Guide to Great Britain*, published in 1901, will set you back the best part of £100, but you can read it for free on openlibrary.org. What I love about these guides is the way they are structured with travel in mind, rather than simply assuming you will go to one place and stay there. They also take for granted that, in order to protect your sense of freedom, you will have very few belongings and, crucially, not be in any kind of rush. In the 'Plan of Tour' section the Great Britain guide proclaims, 'The pedestrian is unquestionably the most independent of travellers' before suggesting what to take in terms of clothing:

> A couple of flannel shirts, a pair of worsted stockings, slippers, the articles of the toilet, a light waterproof, and a stout umbrella will generally be found sufficient equipment…Heavy and complicated knapsacks should be avoided; a light pouch or game-bag is far less irksome, and its position may be shifted at pleasure.

I intend to get some worsted stockings immediately.

Each chapter in the guide is an account of a journey from one place to another – not in a narrative sense, but purely in terms of practical use and local history, architecture and places you can visit along the route. You don't have to do the specified journey because it's structured in a way that means you can read it as both a reference and a narrative book. You get more detailed maps of the major sights, but there's none of the patronising tone that implies not seeing them would make your trip a waste of time. It's a guide for a traveller rather than a tourist.

The chapter 'From Liverpool to London', for example, contains four possible journeys. Just one of these trips includes practical information about Crewe, Rugby, Uttoxeter, Macclesfield, Whitchurch, Stafford, Shrewsbury, Wolverhampton, Walsall, Derby, Nuneaton and Coventry. There are 76 of these chapters, many broken down into three or four different itineraries in this way. This means that wherever you decided to go, you had all the important and useful information we had to wait the best part of a century to get through Google. You can see the bone of the Baedeker approach in modern 'arrival' guides in terms of the ratings system and snatches of history, but the attitude in the original series is pure travel. Even though it's over 100 years old and some of the advice is a little out of date – you can't get to the UK by steamer any more – I'd recommend it to a visitor of these islands far more than a modern guidebook, which I'm becoming convinced teach us only how to travel 'phonetically'.

Back at that wedding, when I went on my first solo slow travel adventure, I did part of my best man's speech in Polish, but rather than attempt to learn it myself I got Agnieszka, the bride, to write it down in phonetic English for me. It cajoled the required laughter out of the Polish half of the audience and raised eyebrows from the English contingent, but I had no real understanding of the gobbledegook I was reading. Nothing about the Polish language perforated my brain and I learned later that I'd rushed a few key passages and that large chunks of it had made no sense at all. I find the same thing happens when I attempt to re-create culinary masterpieces from the pages of cookery books, which only really teach us to cook 'phonetically'. If we follow the instructions exactly, we may well end up eating something that resembles the photograph on the page, but again we have no understanding of the process and thinking behind why we did what we did. It's a short cut, and because it's a short cut if it doesn't work we have no idea where we went wrong. I have 20 cookery books of this kind and I never pick something up from one recipe and apply it to another, because the books teach us only one recipe at a time – there's no real sense of engagement or learning.

In my experience most travel guides work in exactly the same way. They concentrate on short cuts that allow you to experience something foreign, but without any real immersion in the places you go. It's not just travel books and holidays, of course. It seems to be a natural consequence of the way our lives are constantly being sped up – lots of us now only have the time to *live* phonetically too.

This isn't to say that idle travellers don't take any kind of guidebook with them when they go away. I always take books I hope will act as a useful tool to where I'm going – the difference is I pick them for a very specific purpose. I don't want them to tell me what to do or where I should go, but I do expect them to bring my trip alive. I chanced upon this idea a few years ago on a trip to Paris. The first thing to go in my bag was a copy of *The Day of the Jackal* by Frederick Forsyth. For those who haven't come across it, it tells the story of a lone English assassin who is hired by a terrorist group to kill the French President Charles de Gaulle. I'd read it before on a train to Berlin, but wondered whether reading it while travelling to and staying in Paris might give it a more visceral impact.

The result was extraordinary. By the time the Jackal had made it by ferry to France and then by train to Gare du Nord, my Eurostar was pulling into Paris. As

I'd discovered on my way to Poland, long-distance, lone travel changes the way we perceive the world around us, and it makes sense that channelling this altered state into a work of fiction – itself part-mirroring our physical location – will change the way we experience the story. I sat there for a while on a bench reading about how the Jackal made his way to Brussels. Throughout the book his progress is offset by updates with the French police in Paris, who've been tipped off that an unknown English gunman is heading their way. I absorbed the words from the page during rush hour on the Métro, followed by a few hours sitting outside cafés, watching the streets and flinching as government limousines thundered out of the French offices of state. By this stage the quarry had eluded the police by driving into Italy from Switzerland and then up through France. All in time for the Paris-based finale.

I won't ruin it by telling you what happens next, but actually being in the place those last few chapters were set in, and inhaling the frantic excitement of the story on that sunny Friday afternoon, turned the experience into something beyond intoxicating. It allowed Forsyth's words to combine my imagination and reality in a way I could never have got from a conventional guidebook. Yet it was still in a way a guide to Paris. A guide I'm never likely to forget.

Since that experience I've tried the principle in a few other places, with equally evocative results. Agatha Christie wrote a Poirot story called *Evil under the Sun* while staying at the Burgh Island Hotel off the coast of South Devon, near Bigbury-on-Sea. The hotel is an art deco masterpiece, lovingly restored by current owners Deborah Clark and Tony Orchard. The island is tidal, so twice a day you get cut off from the mainland and apart from the hotel there are only a few private houses and a small pub called the Pilchard Inn. There is no mobile phone reception and you'll struggle to find a television. *Evil under the Sun* is set in and around the hotel and because the furniture and décor are of the period (and many of the guests take the opportunity to dress in the fashions of the time) for two days I again found myself blurring the boundaries between imagination and reality. And again, Agatha Christie proved to be a much better guidebook author than the person who wrote the rather exhaustive island biography.

When it comes to overnight trains across Europe there is one author I turn to over and over again, and that's John Le Carré. Heading through Eastern Europe with George Smiley as your companion is a dour experience in some ways, but it is somehow much more enjoyable than reading about his adventures at home on your sofa. Night stops on the train as you delve further into Germany, or through the Alps into Italy, begin to shunt your consciousness in a profound way. For a more modern take, you could also try Robert Ludlum's Jason Bourne series: Bourne is a kind of slow travel superhero because he very rarely seems to go anywhere by plane.

Some people may say that this kind of reading risks destroying the way we enjoy books, which by definition take us back in time, all over the world or out of it entirely, using our own mind. But what I'm describing is simply a way of heightening the experience of reading a book, which wherever you do it ultimately resides only in your own brain.

These alternative guidebooks aren't only tied to fiction, however. One of the greatest travel experiences I've ever had was a 10-day rail trip to Vienna, Budapest and Prague brought alive by three books that combined to give the journey an unshakable status in my memory.

***

It was late February and the mist was dense on the train out of Brussels to Cologne, where my wife Rachel, then-three-year-old Wilf and I would have time for dinner and a brief stop in a LEGO shop before changing for the Deutsche Bahn sleeper service to Vienna. The train trundled through stations that seemed inappropriately grand, vast swathes of concrete offering a historical significance that now appeared misplaced. My knowledge of Belgium, Germany, Austria, Hungary and the Czech Republic had been seared at school by generic analysis of the world wars and the rise of Communism, and I was keen to get beneath this veneer. We went over a wide river and into suburbs, the sun a disc of lurid white trying to burn through the vast expanse of grey. A pink elephant sign for a bar was just visible through the gloom and we charged through red-brick, three-storey houses in rows punctured by Christian minarets and sodden football pitches with unvandalised goals. Woods then nibbled us before a tunnel swallowed us whole.

I was reading *The World of Yesterday* by Stefan Zweig, who had become one of my slow travel heroes after I read his astounding 1926 essay *To Travel or 'Be Travelled'*. Zweig was someone whose views on travel echoed my own. Born in Vienna in 1881, he achieved early acclaim among the literary cafés of the Austrian capital but was keen to prove himself beyond this elite circle and moved first to Berlin and then to Belgium. As a pacifist he worked in the Ministry of War during the First World War and, after the end of the hostilities, excoriated the bloodthirsty tourists who descended on the battlefields of Ypres to buy the luridly painted bullet casings and shells and gawp at fragments of ploughed-up human bone. During the rise of the Nazis he fled to London before moving to the USA, where he found continued fame as a journalist, playwright and author. He was a contemporary of Sigmund Freud and an acclaimed biographer of Balzac, Dickens, Nietzsche and Marie Antoinette. Tragically, he and his wife eventually ended their lives in a suicide pact in Mexico in February 1942 because of the desecration of their beloved Europe and what they saw as the continent's hopeless future.

Travel has often been linked to a kind of spiritual awakening, harking back to a time when it was almost always part of a religious pilgrimage. Zweig's life of travel became a pilgrimage of sorts, albeit one forced on him against his will, forever moving him further from his beloved homeland. As so much of his life was spent on the run from a city he could not return to, travel itself became his home. All of which gives his appreciation and love of travel a heightened edge.

In *To Travel or 'Be Travelled'*, he rails against the emergence of a new kind of tourism that is commonplace today. He starts by explaining how much he loves the railway stations of Europe, how he can sit for hours soaking up the sights, sounds and smells of each 'nation distilled'. He compares them to a new kind of station that has started to appear on the high street, places with no atmosphere that reduce the world into lists of someone else's itineraries – a modern travel agent. He rages against the 'mathematical organisation' they offer by thinking of everything for you in advance and points out that without a role in your own journey you are left with nothing to discover or find out about for yourself.

On group tours people are always on hand to make sure you can't 'stumble into streets where one has no right to be' and Zweig laments the new habit of passing 'before numerous novelties without actually experiencing them at all'. He has little time for 'box tickers' arriving en masse as part of huge tourist groups to visit the major tourist sights: '...what they take home is nothing but the righteous pride of having recorded with their eyes some church, or painting – more a sports record than the sense of any personal maturation and cultural enrichment.' He signs off with an appeal that travel must be preserved as 'an extravagance, a sacrifice to the rules of chance, of daily life to the extraordinary...Only that way can we discover not only the exterior world but also that which lies within us.' It's terrifying to imagine what he'd make of travel today.

The World of Yesterday is Zweig's autobiography, and it tells the story of Europe before, during and after the First World War. It has added poignancy because you read it knowing he took his life soon after it was completed. The Vienna of Zweig's early youth in the late 19th century was the greatest cultural centre in the world, free of prejudice and fear. He expresses this freedom through the city's attitude to speed and time:

> …it was not a century of suffering in which I was born and educated…The rhythm of the new speed had not yet carried over from the machines, the automobile, the telephone, the radio, and the airplane, to mankind; time and age had another measure… Speed was not only thought to be unrefined, but indeed was considered unnecessary…

Wilf's head slipped down my arm and rested in my lap as we charged through the Belgian countryside and Zweig went on to describe how the inhabitants would habitually ignore the great global and political events of the daily newspaper and turn instead to the reports of theatrical productions, concerts and unveiling of great new works of art. Not out of ignorance of global concerns, but from a profound understanding and love of culture in what Zweig calls, retrospectively, a 'tranquil epoch'. He writes of how 'one lived comfortably and stroked one's petty cares as if they were faithful, obedient pets of whom one was not in the least afraid' – and in that sentence you glimpse the state of mind of a man reminiscing of a time before Europe descended into a generation of war.

***

Zweig's memoir gave me an emotional guide to the city of his birth, but it was Carl E Schorske's *Fin-de-siècle Vienna* that put it into a meaningful context. In 1897, the art nouveau movement inspired a group of Viennese artists and architects called the Vienna Secession, who were determined to free the voice and focus of art from the past and into the present. The group's first president was Gustav Klimt and its members included Egon Schiele, Joseph Maria Olbrich and Joseph Hoffmann. Modernism was not restricted to architecture, painting and sculpture. The publication of Freud's *Interpretation of Dreams* in 1899 was part of a wider debate about the nature of the individual. 'Rational man' had conquered nature by understanding the laws of science and harnessing them to propel the industrial age of machines, and through his own sense of moral control. In his exhaustive study of the city at this time, Schorske writes of the 20th century:

> Rational man has had to give place to that richer but more dangerous and mercurial creature, psychological man. This new man is not merely a rational animal, but a creature of feeling and instinct.

Living under a constitutional monarchy and aristocracy that had no respect for youth gave Zweig and his contemporaries little voice for their political frustrations, so they continued to pour their passions into music, literature and art. As a result, art became instilled in Zweig's generation as the highest attainable goal and the ultimate expression of what it meant to be civilised.

***

Reading these two books gave me a combined sense of the hope and tragedy these men wrote of when I found myself orbiting the Ringstrasse in Vienna a few days later. The grand architecture of the city that inspired the young Adolf Hitler felt imposing, and as a typical tourist I would have projected onto this canvas a kind of baffled amazement, seeing within it the sense of grand confidence it was supposed to arouse. But my 'guidebooks' did not imprison me in the tourist's habit of taking everything at face value. With Zweig, Schorske and the Secessionists in my head I was free to empathise with the feeling that when it was built it must have seemed daunting and out of place. The grand building plan was intended to reinvigorate a city that was unsure of where it was going and so sought solace in the architectural classicism of the past. The complaints of the Secessionists make sense to a pedestrian among the vast, impersonal structures that float in the immense boulevards designed – like those of Paris – to aid the military should they need to crush popular dissent: huge stone staircases, raised balustrades and columns creating impenetrable stone islands in an ocean of tarmac and cobbled stone.

In reality, the tragedy of Vienna's political future was already in motion, with the rise of anti-Semitism in the form of Karl Lueger, who became mayor in 1897. Lueger's successful political model, partly utilising the middle class (and Jewish) obsession with art, culture and commerce as proof of their distance from the concerns of the working class, was something else that would later inspire Hitler. The more the middle classes concentrated on culture, the further they got from political power; they watched the mass demonstrations from Czech and Slav nationalists, socialists and Christian Social anti-Semites with increasing alarm. Suddenly, in the context of his own tragic hindsight, Zweig's lament for Vienna and his eventual suicide begin to make sense. The forward-looking, passionate cultural hopes for the new kind of man he and his peers sought to create were to be side-stepped before being crushed during both world wars by the very human behaviour their artistic passion had hoped to defeat.

We jogged out of the way of tourists being pulled in ornate, horse-drawn carts, and found some of the cafés deep inside the city where Zweig and his contemporaries would have sat and talked. Most of these places have become touristified, but that's not a problem for three-year-old boys whose eyes are widened by mesmerising brightly coloured cakes. Klimt's *Kiss* is now in a palace to the south of the city called the Belvedere, home of Archduke Franz Ferdinand whose assassination sparked the outbreak of the First World War. We walked there, drifting aimlessly through the ornate gardens so Wilf could balance carefully on the walls that were lined with hedges, before he charged defiantly into the middle of a flock of pigeons minding their own business on the grass. When we eventually made it into the gallery, the paintings of Shiele and Klimt appeared apologetic in the kind of building the artists themselves were resisting in their work.

I'm not attempting to claim that I became an expert on Vienna in those four days, or that I found out some mystical truth about the city a guidebook could never have revealed. Simply that the two books I chose to guide me through a snapshot of the city's history allowed me to make sense of my visit through my own interests and curiosity. The only 'must see' we visited was Klimt's *Kiss*. We could have spent a fortune on opera tickets, or ploughed our way through the no doubt marvellous museums to try to extract an essence of the city, but instead we toured the various playgrounds that Wilf excitedly pointed out from the tram windows and pottered about, allowing serendipity and the words of my guides to show us around instead. No guilt, no 'making the most' of our stay – just a few days' walking and reading a couple of books when Wilf was asleep.

In retrospect my conclusions are probably simplistic, but in my mind Vienna now has a meaningful sense of place. I treasure my memories of Wilf leaning against the glass of Café Central staring at the exotic cakes, but when I think of Vienna I don't think of tragedy or a lost cultural relevance. Nor do I think of a nondescript museum I trudged through out of a false sense of duty.

I see Zweig as a young man, representing the unashamed artistic hope of humanity and I love the fact that *he* was my guide to the city *he* was born in and the city *he* adored. This also puts Zweig's slightly forceful, impassioned plea for the value of *real* travel into its proper context. He understood what it was like to lose your home, which is the one anchor all travel relies on.

The Secessionists eventually gave a definition for Modern Man as someone 'condemned to re-create his own universe', which is surely what Zweig was forced to do. It gives further support to the idea that travel, like reading, ultimately takes place only in your brain. My guidebooks had an added bonus, too. Being able to place the concept of Modernism and the name of Sigmund Freud into a context like *fin-de-siècle* Vienna allowed me to make sense of things I had previously shuffled over with only an assumption of understanding. Walking through the streets among those impenetrable buildings brought the need for Modernism alive in me in a way no television programme, school lesson or book could have hoped to elicit. I was almost jealous of the Secessionists for having something as physically imposing as the Ringstrasse to rally against. Those men and women must have revelled in a new and profound idea of the purpose of being young. Regardless of what was to happen later, the idea that this charge of cultural excitement was being led by people like Klimt, Hofmannsthall, Kokoschka, Schiele and Wagner puts our own popular cultural heroes to shame. I certainly left Vienna with a fresh understanding of old ideas, and for me that is one of the purposes of travel.

***

It was a Saturday morning when we left for Budapest on a train ultimately headed for Belgrade. For some reason this gave me a sense of foreboding. The further east in Europe you go, the less pretentious and more civilised the trains become – the ubiquitous proud, suited waiters certainly shame the trolleys on UK trains. The seats were low behind our heads, which opened up the carriage to more natural light and smiles from old ladies, although I'm sure those were intended for Wilf. As the beginnings of a blizzard drifted from the sky I pointed out two hares charging in a field alongside the line. The beaten, brown landscape was soon obliterated by snow, but the train trundled on.

We came to a large station with no platform, and waited for a seemingly never-ending freight train to pull empty cargo crates, perhaps to be filled again by the sweatshops of the East. Slow travel really does take you through each nation's 'back stage'. As we waited the sun broke through the thick black cloud, lighting up snowflakes as gusts of wind puffed powdered snow in circles along the ground. Two aggressive-looking policemen then began patrolling the train and I was reminded of words of warning from my faster travelling friends: 'You're taking a three-year-old on trains across Hungary and Slovakia? Are you sure?' The men began questioning passengers and I noticed their guns and folded visibility vests tucked neatly in their belts. Then the train began to move and the policemen decided to search the toilet together – for quite some time.

Three-year-olds have insatiable curiosity. It's one of the things I love most about children. It's as though everything that exists in the world has been put there for them to ask questions about and try to understand, which of course is completely correct. It's only adults who no longer see such simple truths. Having a three-year-old guide your eyes through a train window, instead of the other way round, is worth doing too. Somewhere between Vienna and the border with Hungary the number of windmills increase to the point where they are the only thing you can think about. Wilf insisted on calling them 'mind mills', which was briefly endearing. I pushed him for an explanation but he wafted me away and pulled out some paper and his colouring pens and began to draw the endless sheds of what I assumed were battery chicken farms in unremarkable fields. We had cleared the snow now and he paused for a moment to ask, 'Why is everything brown?' It was February and he was right. The countryside stuck to a pallet of colour seen through a veil of brown. The greens were brown, the reds were brown and the yellows were brown, which made the bright yellow and blue houses defiantly beautiful.

Once you've been on a night train, every train journey that follows feels ludicrously short in comparison. The station in Budapest came too quickly and we covered ourselves in woollen gloves, scarves and hats before climbing down and outside. Sometimes idle travellers make mistakes, and Budapest in February turned out to be one of mine. A few hours later we crossed the Danube in a punishing wind and Wilf began crying because his 'face hurt'. So I stopped a taxi and we had soon set up camp in our hotel room, drinking hot chocolate and eating chocolate biscuit cake with Hungarian-dubbed *Thomas the Tank Engine* on the TV.

I thought it might have warmed up the next morning when we left for the outdoor Szechenyi Baths, the largest bathhouse in Europe, with its own station on the Metro line. It was a steady minus two degrees but surely we'd get warm towels and thick dressing gowns to shield us from the cold once inside? I paid the fee and walked with Wilf (not Rachel, who was busy taking photographs for a newspaper article) into a steamy labyrinth. We got down to our trunks in one of the changing rooms that turned out to be our locker too. I took a small octagonal token with a number on it to the man in a white coat, white shorts, white socks and yellow flip-flops standing in the nearest kiosk. He made lots of gestures that seemed to imply forgetting the number would not be a smart move. We had a very confused non-conversation because the number on my metal octagon did not correspond to the number of our changing room, but eventually I worked out that this was a deliberate way to befuddle any potential thief. He seemed quite angry, but I chose to ignore it.

We walked into the green-tiled complex, looking for the outside bath area where we'd find old men playing chess amid the steam. It wasn't long before other people started to stare at me angrily, but I still had no idea why. After walking through what seemed like a slightly decrepit greenhouse we made it outside

– wearing only our trunks, in minus two degrees. It seemed sensible for us to get into the pool where the chess-playing chaps were as quickly as possible, but by the time I'd walked there – the frozen tiles stinging my heel and toes – I realised how cold it was. I held Wilf close in a bear hug and slowly got into the pool. Then after a bit of shivering dithering I remembered I was the adult and we took the plunge. It was deeper than I expected, or we were higher than I expected. Either way the large tidal wave of water we created rather ruined a game of chess two old men were playing a few yards away. By the time I realised this and began making the universal facial signs of apology, Wilf was screaming because the water was too hot. So we got out again and then we discovered how cold it *really* was. He didn't cry, bless him – it was probably too cold for his tear ducts to activate – but his body was shaking and his lips were blue. Lots of old ladies began shouting at me, presumably asking where the hell his mother was.

We'd nearly made it back inside the steamy warmth of the building when we were accosted by an angry man in a white coat, white shorts, white socks and green flip-flops who apparently wanted to know why we were walking around his bathhouse in bare feet. There is an international loathing of verrucas, it seems.

Once I'd negotiated another wordless apology, we found a large green pool inside and began using strange blue dumbbells to swirl round and round in the water. We did as many revolutions as I felt were required to prevent the experience being a total disaster. When we got out I went back to the kiosk and had, thankfully, remembered the number, so we were able to get our clothes but discovered they didn't supply towels. I had to stand a shivering Wilf next to a radiator outside our cubicle and dry both of us with my shirt and T-shirt. On our way out a man behind another kiosk came up, gave me a partial refund and shouted something at me, neither of which I understood.

***

The next day we were back at the station for a seven-hour train journey to Prague that left at 9am. Thankfully the train was warm and, as it was the return of the previous night's overnight service from Berlin, there was literally no one on it apart from us. I'd be lying if I said a seven-hour train journey during the day with a three-year-old didn't have the potential to be a bit grim, but slow travel is all about looking through inconvenience and thinking a little differently.

Back then, Wilf had a two-hour nap in the middle of the day, so I set myself the task of tiring him out to ensure I had some time with my next guidebook, *Vaclav Havel* by John Keane. You'd be amazed what you can do to entertain a small child when you have the run of an entirely empty train. I have spent literally hundreds of pounds on lurid child-centred attractions in my life and none of them has ever made him happier or laugh more than he did that morning. I christened each carriage with the behaviours you had to perform while you were in them as we walked the length of the train. The carriage immediately behind us was the 'dancing' carriage, so we leapt about a fair amount in that one. One of the best things that can happen to a three-year-old, or a 33-year-old for that matter, is for a 33-year-old to start dancing for no logical reason at all. I have no photographs of the three of us bouncing around in that carriage, but I will never need any.

Behind that we came to the 'upside-down' carriage, where small children had to remain upside down the entire time they were in it – he *really* loved that one. After that we had the 'eating crisps and sweets' carriage and the 'Daddy falls asleep' carriage, but we kept having to go back to the 'dancing' and 'jumping off the seats' ones. By the time I'd run out of ideas, Wilf was exhausted and I began to stare out the window as he dozed off on my lap.

My guidebook called itself a biography of Vaclav Havel, but it was much more than that. Havel's life story began in an independent republic. As a toddler he suffered the rule of the Nazis before enduring four decades of Communist totalitarian rule, all of which would have horrified Zweig. But this 'modern man', an author and playwright, used his personality, and his art, in a way Zweig and his contemporaries had literally dreamed of, to become the figurehead for the Velvet Revolution of 1989 and President of the newly formed Czech Republic.

Until I read Keane's book, I felt I had become so hardened to the horrors of the Second World War and the activities of the Nazis that I had little to learn and little shock left to feel. As I write, I can see how insulting that is, because when you think about it the cultural shortcuts of films, documentaries or photographs offer only a false sense of drama and empathy. I found the combination of my own curiosity and this guidebook got hold of me in a way I hadn't come close to experiencing before.

Havel was born into an affluent family in 1936. He described himself in his early years as a 'pampered bourgeois child' and great things were certainly expected of him. But 18 months into his life Hitler annexed Austria, and the Western powers seemed content to let him, assuming that the Führer was interested only in reuniting German-speaking lands. On 15 September 1938, British Prime Minister Neville Chamberlain went for talks with Hitler, who advised him that Germany now demanded the right to secede the Sudetenland from Czechoslovakia. Chamberlain told him he would consider his request carefully, but on 23 September Hitler went ahead and announced both the annexation and the evacuation of non-Germans from the Sudetenland with five days' notice.

When Havel was five years old, Reinhard Heydrich, Hitler's favoured successor, was installed in Prague and set about imposing martial law to compensate for what Hitler saw as the soft treatment the Czechs had received so far. Hitler described Heydrich as having a 'heart of iron'. It was Heydrich who was the architect of *Kristallnacht* – a night of violence and murder aimed at Jews across Germany and Austria that culminated in 30,000 being sent to concentration camps; it is now considered to be the first act of the Holocaust. As soon as Heydrich arrived in Prague the Gestapo began making mass arrests and performing summary executions to terrify the local population. Intellectuals were targeted, universities closed, students arrested and the most high-profile victims shot while what remained of the country fell under the grip of Nazism. Keane writes: 'The essence of totalitarian power was terror – soul- and body-destroying fear driven by the expectation that death and destruction...were just around the corner.' The mass slaughter of Jews and Romany Gipsies in concentration camps or dumped in mass forest graves had begun.

The Czechs began to fear that they would be next, but Heydrich had a different future in mind for them. While those who would not fit in with the Germanic ideal, or were undesirable, would indeed be liquidated, the rest would become German. Hitler made a speech in the same year (1941) that laid out how this national deletion would be achieved. Within 20 years he wanted to push the Czech language 'back to the importance of a dialect'. He sought to kill their nationality by destroying their language and Heydrich, later dubbed the Butcher of Prague, was the man to make it happen.

I stared out of the window to take this thought in. We were into Slovakia now, cutting through woodland; I saw small groups of men, tramps I suppose, warming themselves in the cold around various fires along the side of the track. Wilf was snoring on my lap and Rachel had curled herself up on a long, plush, red bench seat. We slowed almost to a stop, as though the train had suffered a power cut, and I saw the dishevelled men drinking moonshine from unbranded green bottles. They were talking and laughing. The train sped up.

I went back to the book to consider that thought again. Hitler intended to kill the Czech language. Why? Because ultimately he knew that would cut the people off from the unique concepts and ideas their language contained, and in so doing destroy their connection to their ancestors, their myths, their history and the complex way all these things combined to build their sense of who and what they were. Hitler knew that by forcing them to adopt German he would – by controlling that language though propaganda – literally be able to change the capacity of the Czech population to think. Within a few generations his work would be done and the Czech identity would be at best a memory, at worst non-existent. Presumably his aim would have been to roll out this principle across all European nations in the eventual 'Fourth Reich'. Stefan Zweig was still alive when Hitler made this speech, and you can only imagine how keenly he would have felt the horror of all it implied.

We were soon into the hills of the modern-day Czech Republic. The rivers were frozen but once we'd lost some height I noticed a few brave anglers on the banks, casting into the small patches of running water that were visible. The colour pallet began to change and I started to see orange and bright yellow among the metronomic greens and browns. We cut between large white buildings and churches with Tiffany-blue spires and mini domes – the wooded hills and flashes of colour ushering us into Bohemia. By the time Wilf and Rachel woke up half an hour later I'd learned something astonishing about Heydrich and there was a 'sight' in Prague I now desperately wanted to visit.

The next morning we headed out to find the small and apparently unremarkable Church of St Cyril and St Methodius, not far from an apartment Havel's family once owned. The church was tucked away on a side street a long way from Charles Bridge and Prague Castle and we found ourselves walking down residential roads away from the main shopping streets. Backing onto one of these roads I spotted some small holes around what looked like a large letterbox-shaped opening in the wall beneath a grey plaque. This was the place we were looking for.

The holes were made by bullets fired by 700 SS soldiers who spent a day and a night trying to kill the Czech soldiers and resistance fighters who had assassinated Reinhard Heydrich in the summer of 1942. It was the final act of Operation Anthropoid, a daring plan devised by the exiled Czech government and British Special Operations Executive (founded by Winston Churchill in 1940 for the purpose of espionage, sabotage and reconnaissance). Czech nationals Jozef Gabčík and Jan Kubiš had parachuted into Czechoslovakia with seven other soldiers, including one named Karel Čurda, and made their way to Prague, where they joined up with resistance fighters. On 27 May they confronted Heydrich's car on its way to Prague Castle. Gabčík stood in front of it, intending to open fire, but his gun jammed, so Kubiš threw an anti-tank grenade. It landed next to the car and exploded. Heydrich, apparently unhurt, fired and gave chase before collapsing. The assassins, assuming their plot had failed, ran for it. It took Heydrich a week to die from his injuries, but in that time investigations were swift and reprisals were brutal. Čurda gave away their hiding place in the crypt in return for a half-million Reichsmark reward and the Nazis descended on the church, determined to make an example of the Czech nationals who had dared to rise against them.

Today you can go down into the crypt, where a small display of photographs takes you through the operation and its aftermath. Estimates of the number of people killed by the Nazis in revenge for Heydrich's death number between 3,000 and 5,000. The worst atrocity took place in the village of Lidice, which was razed to the ground when the investigation falsely 'proved' that they had given sanctuary to the assassins. All 199 men of the village were executed and nearly 300 women and children were sent to concentration camps.

On the far wall of the crypt you can see the hole the men were desperately trying to excavate to take them through to the city's sewer system that would have given them their freedom. They chiselled at it all night while the SS soldiers bombarded them with gunfire, gas, grenades and finally water in a desperate attempt to drown them out. Early the next morning the SS men heard two shots and then there was silence. Having exhausted their ammunition the last two survivors – Kubiš and Gabčík – had used their two remaining bullets on themselves. It was discovered later that they were 12 inches from breaking through the stone and making their escape. The brutality of the reprisals was such that it was hard to count the operation as a success, but the assassination of the highest ranking Nazi official in the entire war had an impact on the Allies' morale. After the war, Čurda attempted suicide but failed, and was later hanged in Prague for treason.

Standing in that crypt among the story and those photographs is one of the travel memories I know I haven't fully understood yet. It's an experience that followed me home and pops up every so often in my head. We left feeling sad but strangely proud that we'd stumbled on a story that reflected the triumph of the human spirit in the face of such seemingly impossible odds.

***

Three years after the Nazis had been defeated Czechoslovakia fell to a Stalin-backed Communist putsch and became part of the Eastern Bloc. Vaclav Havel was 12. The subsequent dictatorship lasted 41 years, but he somehow managed to emerge from it as a free, democratically elected President of the Czech Republic. The story of how he got there is too long to tell here, but what I find astonishing about his story is the bloody-minded bravery that inspired him to put his life at risk by staging secret performances of his own and others' plays. Like Hitler, he knew the value of language and ideas, and would not allow the voice of his nation to be defeated. He also co-wrote *Charter* 77, published in 1977, a manifesto for change that the government banned, labelling its authors 'traitors and renegades' before sending the most prominent signatories, including Havel, to prison for five years.

Havel campaigned more openly on his release in the 1980s and after the Berlin Wall came down on 9 November 1989 the Czech people were ready to march. Theatres and libraries were turned into crucibles of democracy and became forums for debate. Stages were turned over to the audience, who used them for public meetings. Actors and students went on strike and took to the streets. As the final days of the revolution approached, libraries effectively overturned rules on censorship by releasing banned, anti-government books. Mass strikes were organised and up to 800,000 people flocked to demonstrate on the streets. Eventually the Communist government stepped down after the bloodless Velvet (or Gentle, as it's known to Slovaks) Revolution and Havel was elected President on 29 December. Zweig would have rejoiced.

We found some of the theatres where the adrenaline of change had been channelled into revolution and walked up Petrin Hill, where the young Havel and his contemporaries had discussed their hopes and dreams. I looked down on the city and, although I knew I'd discovered only a tiny fraction of its recent history, I felt I'd learned enough to recognise the suffering, strength and pride that existed in the air between the buildings and cobbled streets. On the train back to London I knew the trip had changed my preconceptions of each city and Eastern Europe as a whole. My guides had helped me access new ideas and understanding that would stay with me long after I got home.

***

I thought of Wilf, Rachel and me walking on Petrin Hill when I heard the news that Havel had died on 18 December 2011. His obituaries reflected on his political life, rather than his life as a writer, and implied that he was somehow unconscious of the decisions that forced him into such a crucial national role. It was as though he were travelling through his life using a kind of instinctive map. I read the various obituaries voraciously, trying to get a sense of finality about his life. Then I dug out my copy of John Keane's book and found a quote from Havel himself that confirms the view of a man without a coherent plan, simply following his own instincts. Writing while in prison of the decision to publicly co-author *Charter* 77 he said: 'We never decided that we would go to jail. In fact, we never decided to become dissidents…We simply went ahead and did certain things that we felt we ought to do, and that seemed to us decent to do, nothing more or less.'

I chanced upon a poem by a contemporary of Havel – the Czech poet Miroslav Holub – while reading the news of Havel's death. I have a suspicion that it might actually be about him and, rather serendipitously, it also encapsulates a few of my thoughts about guidebooks in the kind of ultra-efficient way only a true poet can. The poem is called *Brief Thoughts On Maps* and it appeared in *The Times Literary Supplement* on 4 February

1977 – a month after Havel and his co-authors published *Charter 77*.

The young lieutenant of a small Hungarian
detachment in the Alps
sent a reconnaissance unit out onto the icy
wasteland.
It began to snow
immediately,
snowed for two days and the unit
did not return.
The lieutenant suffered:
he had dispatched
his own people to death.

But the third day the unit came back.
Where had they been? How had they made
their way?
Yes, they said, we considered ourselves
lost and waited for the end. And then one of us
found a map in his pocket. That calmed us down.
We pitched camp, lasted out the snowstorm and
then with the map
we discovered our bearings.
And here we are.

The lieutenant borrowed this remarkable map
and had a good look at it. It was not a map of
the Alps
but of the Pyrenees.

Chapter 4

Embrace disaster

An inconvenience is only an adventure wrongly considered
G K Chesterton, 'On Running After One's Hat'

In the opening pages of *In Patagonia*, Bruce Chatwin recalls a cabinet in his grandmother's house that contained a small piece of skin with tufts of red hair apparently taken from a brontosaurus. His grandmother's cousin, Charley Milward, had found the preserved carcass in a cave in Patagonia and shipped it to the British Museum for closer examination. Unfortunately it rotted on the boat, but the small piece he sent to his cousin through the post remained intact. As a child Chatwin became fixated both by it and by South America. The latter was a long way from his childhood home and he filled the idea of it with fantasies of monsters. He finally made it to 'the end of the world' at 34 and the book tells of his quest to find the exact place where the preserved dinosaur skin was discovered. The 'brontosaurus' turned out to be a Mylodon, but the monster was surely just the bait that enticed the boy to wander and wonder through a landscape that would help make his name as a man.

We all have places we're planning to visit 'one day', at some uncertain point in the future; like Chatwin, lots of us head off in search of a specific kind of bait, or inspired by one, only for the real purpose of our quest to emerge after we've been lured in. In my case it was not a piece of dinosaur skin, but a feather from a golden eagle stuck on my bedroom wall that I was given as a memento by a falconer I met in Scotland a few years ago. He had briefly allowed me to have the golden eagle to which the feather belonged on my fist – another moment when my perception of time began to change. 'Awesome' is a word I habitually use, but in this instance it reclaimed its proper meaning. No matter how often you are told a bird of prey never uses its beak to attack – it dispatches its quarry with its taloned feet – when a golden eagle stands on your fist with its beak a few inches from your nose it's impossible not to find your innards crumbling. There was no trace of conscience in the vital yellow eyes that flicked from my face to the sky and then back, rather disconcertingly, to my left cheek.

The immense weight of the eagle weakened my arm and, sensing that her perch might give way, she slowly extended her wings for balance; the span of brown and white feathers opened further behind me than my head could turn. I was utterly lost in the moment – to be so close to such a majestic, wild creature was both riveting and terrifying. As I had long suspected, eagles not only give you a rare glimpse of the natural world, but can give a whole new perspective on the inner world, too.

Humans have been mesmerised by birds of prey for

millennia and the practice of falconry is surely the ultimate expression of this fascination. Raptors (such as eagles, which hunt prey on the ground or water) and falcons (which usually hunt in the air) are generally rather lazy, which could be another reason why I'm so fond of them. Their motto seems to be 'minimum effort, maximum effect'. When they see potential prey they are able to calculate instinctively whether the reward for taking their quarry will be worth the effort they'll expend in catching it. I've been out hunting with Harris hawks and they'll turn their beaks up at a vole right by your feet if it's too small, or a plump rabbit that they deem too far away. Once they have caught their prey the falconer shows them a titbit of food (which is safer for the bird to eat on account of its not being alive and therefore offering no risk of injury). The falconer then dispatches the prey and puts it in his bag to eat himself (or to give to the falcon) when he gets home.

The earliest known reference to falconry is from around 700 BC and the training required and equipment needed are largely unchanged since that time. The sport seems to have originated in China and spread west across the deserts of Asia to the Middle East and Africa before claiming the imagination of Europe, too. Falconry is referred to in the writings of Arabic astronomers, Saxon poetry, ancient stories of the Japanese Samurai and, of course, tales of our own Knights of the Round Table. In the mountains of Kazakhstan today you'll still find men and their sons on horseback, hunting for foxes and small deer with golden eagles on the fist. At the age of 16 the boys are sent down a rope to the eagle's eyrie on a cliff face to take a juvenile bird. They train it in its natural behaviour for six months and it then becomes their companion for the next nine years. After that they release it back into the wild, where it can live for a further 20 years (though it can survive up to 80 in captivity).

Falconry is often lumped in with other blood sports, but the reason it's so alluring to me is the proximity it gives you to completely natural, wild behaviour and the way your own perceptions slow down as you're led by the bird's instincts. Within hours you'll find yourself noticing small mammals in the undergrowth that you usually simply blunder through. It's also an equal relationship. Birds of prey stay with a falconer only as long as he remains a more efficient food source than they would find in the wild. 'Bad' falconers are often rewarded by their expensive birds simply flying away.

Despite many close experiences with all kinds of birds of prey, I had, until recently, never gone out to look for eagles in their natural habitat. When I looked at the feather on my wall I was acutely aware I had never seen them as conquerors of their own domain. I think they inspire me precisely because they are not exotic, like the animals that roam the African plain, but more a living, breathing manifestation of Britain's ancient landscape. They had come to represent a part of myself I knew existed but had never got round to visiting or understanding.

In terms of statistics, both geologically and climatically, Britain is an island of averages. This perhaps explains why grand scenery and better weather are the two things we most often seek in other countries. But when it comes to eagles we are high in the global league table. The island of Mull in Scotland has the highest density of eagles anywhere in Europe, and although it might not seem as hard to get to as Patagonia, it took me and my companion Kevin Parr twice as long to get there by train, bus and ferry as it would have taken to fly from London to Buenos Aires. That might make it sound like a total nightmare, but to the idle traveller it suggests that getting to Mull from London by rail, road and ferry is a greater feat of personal exploration than getting to South America by air. Slow travel is not about haste and distance, after all – it's about reflection and depth.

With Chatwin in mind, I asked my old friend and fellow bird-of-prey fan Kev if he would come with me to try to find a golden eagle in its natural habitat. In the past he and I have quite literally gone on wild goose chases to find unusual birds that arrive in the UK having got lost on migration. I don't know about you, but I find something fascinating and comforting about nature sometimes getting things wrong. We once drove six hours to Cornwall before dawn on a Saturday on the off chance of seeing a lost snowy owl (the first wild one to be recorded in the UK since 1957).

Finding himself between jobs, Kev immediately suggested we head for Mull. By the time I hung up the phone we had decided to get the overnight train to Glasgow from London on a Thursday night, make the three-hour connection from Glasgow to Oban by train the next morning and finally take the ferry to Craignure on Mull. It would be dark by the time we arrived, but then we would have the entire Saturday to go looking for eagles before making the return journey on the Sunday. Admittedly it was December and there would be only eight hours of daylight, but that was deliberate. Less light, but also fewer tourists. I would arrive back in London at seven o'clock on Monday morning, in time for work.

I was nervously excited at the prospect of finally seeing eagles in the wild, although it soon transpired we would be very lucky to see any at all. As much as the eagles, though, I was looking forward to spending some time with an old friend. I had not seen Kev in almost a year, and even then it had been a few snatched words over pints before and after a football match. He had regaled me with stories of childhood holidays in Mull and countless eagle sightings throughout our lives and now, finally, I was heading there myself.

I was busy in London with meetings and a party to help organise when he called to say that our trip might not go entirely to plan. He began cackling over the phone.

'Have you seen the weather?'

'Er, no,' I replied. 'Too busy with this party. When are you getting here?'

Kev stifled another laugh. 'I'm on the train, get into Paddington in about an hour, but the weather in Scotland...' he paused. 'It said on the news it's the worst storm in recorded history. Winds of 165 miles per hour, which is the same as a category five hurricane. There's a red weather warning. People are being advised to cancel *all* travel.'

'Ah,' was the only response I could muster.

He laughed a little more. '*And* there's no power in Oban or Mull and the ferries have been cancelled. They reckon over 60,000 people north of Glasgow have no electricity.'

Surprised, but unfazed – as you've probably noticed by now, slow travel rarely goes exactly according to plan – I asked if the sleeper train was still running from London.

'Yes, that seems to be OK. We should be able to get as far as Glasgow.'

We met up an hour or so later in a pub in Soho and were soon laughing at the ridiculousness of what we were about to attempt, but it didn't occur to either of us to cancel the trip. Kev and I met when we were still at school over 20 years ago. There's a kind of friendship you can only forge around that age, when you are defined by little more than your dreams, the music you listen to and the girls you desperately want to kiss. As is the nature of life, we rarely saw each other now that children and responsibilities had intervened, but when we did there was never any recrimination over the lack of phone calls, emails or birthday cards in between. Our friendship operated on a more elemental level.

We moved on to the party, which was beautifully surreal – a mix of '80s pop stars and the accountants, lawyers and builders their contemporaries had grown into. The news that we were about to head off in search of eagles was greeted with wide eyes and an impulsive plea to come too. We emerged a few hours later, flushed with booze on empty stomachs, and went in search of a taxi that would take us to our beds and the next part of our journey, the First ScotRail sleeper to Glasgow from Euston.

Sleeper services run every day apart from Saturdays direct from London to Glasgow, Edinburgh, Aberdeen, Inverness and Fort William (and many smaller stations in between). Ours would get to Glasgow in around seven hours. I'd done a similar journey to Inverness a few years before to see whether you could cross the north coast of Scotland on public transport. It is almost possible. You can get a free return taxi from the station at Thurso to John O'Groats and then hitch a ride with what's known as the post bus from Thurso as far as Tongue. It's literally a minibus the postman drives to do his deliveries and you can cadge a lift for less than a fiver. Post-bus routes go all over the Highlands, giving locals and walkers a vital link between isolated towns and villages. On that sleeper to Inverness you wake up in the morning as the train climbs its way through the Cairngorms, which is as good a way to greet the morning as I've ever experienced. The best part of our journey up the west coast would be the connection from Glasgow to Oban. It's not uncommon for people to go to Oban for the day just to experience the countryside in between.

It took 20 minutes to find a taxi on Shaftesbury Avenue, which was unnerving in the extreme. By the time we finally flagged one down we had only 15 minutes before the train left Euston. As both of us are childhood and lifelong fans of *Lord of the Rings,* Kev joked that our trip was destined to match the triumphs and disasters of Frodo and Sam into Mordor, where the eagles would surely appear at the end in the nick of time. The train bar would be our Rivendell.

We ran madly and managed to get on before the scheduled time of departure, only to find the service was suffering at least an hour's delay. We found a seat in the bar carriage and took huge joy in unfolding the 375 Explorer map of Mull I'd brought along. There was a single 'main' road that circumnavigated most of the island and a few smaller tracks ducking off it now and then, but the vast majority of Mull has proved impossible to tame, even on foot, because so much of it is bog and marshland. I stared at it excitedly but had nothing to bring it to life beyond my imagination. Kev stared at it while smiling the kind of knowing smile I'd seen on his face so many times before. After a few glasses of Deuchars IPA we stumbled giggling to our separate compartments before slumping into soft duvet and thick blanket-laden beds. As someone cursed with the burden of commuting a few times a week, the idea of being able to lie down in a bed on a train and have a proper sleep, as opposed to the haunting semi-conscious state as you flirt with missing your stop, was perhaps the greatest drunken luxury I could have hoped to find. I was consumed with sleep and dreamed of eagles.

Meanwhile, Scotland continued to be battered by extreme weather. The reported 165mph winds had hit the Cairngorms and a wind turbine in Ayrshire had exploded and caught fire. Town centres were closed to protect people from falling debris, and articulated lorries had been turned over in the ferocious winds. By the time our train got to Glasgow at eight in the morning all train services up into the north of Scotland had been cancelled. That last piece of information hadn't reached us when we arrived late into Glasgow Central Station and desperately hailed a taxi to take us to our connection from Glasgow Queen Street at 8.21. The concourse was full of stranded travellers, all in varying degrees of frustration. Our only hope of getting to Oban was a bus the rail company was hoping to provide, assuming the roads were open. All Oban-bound passengers were collected in a waiting room and furnished with free coffee and tea. Kev was now looking a little grim. While he was prepared to embrace the slow travel methodology, he is notorious for being car sick unless he's the one driving, and the prospect of three hours on a bus was clearly troubling him. I suggested we hire a car from the nearest airport instead and his eyes brightened, but only briefly.

'No, that'll cost a fortune and we can't take it on the ferry to Mull, we haven't booked in advance.' He went off and bought multiple bottles of water and Lucozade, before explaining he would not be much of a companion for the next stage of the journey. 'The only way I can do it without puking is if I sit by a window and try to go to sleep. It's best if you don't talk to me.'

Kev winced as we lurched our way out of the city but I was thrilled to be inconvenienced so quickly. I'm sure you've noticed that once disaster strikes most travellers are consumed by a kind of inevitable camaraderie. Some people can't cope and freak out at the lack of predictable control, but the majority begin to chat and joke to strangers in a way that would have been impossible if things had gone to plan. It's almost as if subconsciously they're slightly relieved that things have gone awry. I was a little frustrated that I would miss seeing the landscape from a widescreen train window, but a quick look on Google maps told me the road and rail routes were almost identical. Kev had also insisted on sitting immediately behind the stairs to the toilet, making our window much wider than most.

Our co-travellers included lots of overnight Christmas shoppers; two adventurers of the kind you usually see when you flirt with the edges of the earth, both carrying rucksacks that reached far above their heads and almost as far down as the backs of their knees; a couple who looked a little lost; and a clutch of old ladies who unfurled their knitting with the kind of no-nonsense resolve you'd expect. Chatwin's travels always seem to unearth presidents and lost maidens with countless memorable quips, but the conversations and comments I overheard on the bus were far more mundane. One of the knitters shouted, 'If anyone else asks me to move before Oban they're dead!' after the man next to her indicated he wanted to change seats. Phone calls around us revealed our companions' shocked responses to the travel chaos, and soon mangled cars had begun to appear in ditches and splayed about trees on the roadsides.

On a bus the view from the window and the scenery pulls you in completely, far more so than on a train, because there is nowhere else to look. We drove beyond Dumbarton, and Glasgow slipped away. A couple of days later we would return by train at night, and the red and orange glow of Greenock would seem as violent as an unstoppable lava flow forcing us back into the metropolis – and normal life – along the Clyde. That morning glimpses of impressive geology only hinted at what was to come. The clouds were grey and relentless, and at 9am the earth had only recently turned far enough to bring the sun into view as we hugged the length of Loch Lomond. The top of Ben Lomond was barely visible behind the cloud, but already you could sense that a different attitude was to be found among this mountainous landscape.

These early peaks would turn out to be the gates to another new perspective, but it wasn't until we'd stopped for a break at the services in Tyndale that the trip really pulled us in. Here the pine trees and steep mountainsides were covered in snow, and we all had to walk through pools of sludge to get to the shop and café. Having forgotten about my phone so far that morning I checked my email and Twitter to see what had unfolded at the party after we'd gone. I had a few messages intimating that they thought the trip in search of eagles had been taken as an elaborate and inebriated joke. Text messages of intrigue came from other quarters, asking questions about the train journey. There were missed calls and answerphone messages from unfamiliar numbers too, but I couldn't face listening to those. I tried to Tweet a photograph of the snow-covered mountains but I lost reception somewhere between the coach and the shop. I retraced my steps, but it had gone. Phone, Twitter and email would have to do without me for a while.

As the coach followed the contours of the snow-dappled scene of mountain, forest, scrubland, the calm water of the lochs and the distant sight of waterfalls, everything seemed perfectly beautiful but almost eerie. Each corner we turned seemed to reveal the tops of another mountain or a pristine angle I hadn't previously seen. The road became invisible once we'd travelled each stretch of it, immediately absorbed back into the sweeping arc of the geography. The water in one of the many lochs we drove along was so still that even through the lurching coach window I could take photos of perfect reflections between the water and steep banks of snow-covered scree. Further on the trees became so thickly covered with lichen that I thought they were in leaf. A bright green, silvery growth flaked all over the trunks and branches, even the thinnest ones. It looked as though a clumsy giant had absent-mindedly covered them in lurid foil. It all contributed to a sense that something strange was at work.

One of my favourite stories about travel that explores the relationship between our desires and what we can attain in the real world is an often-ignored work by Edgar Allan Poe called, rather fittingly for this trip, *The Domain of Arnheim* (Land of Eagles). It's usually dismissed as a slightly peculiar homage to landscape gardening, but the last story he ever wrote, *Landor's*

Cottage, is described as 'a pendant to the *Domain of Arnheim*', which has always intrigued me. If the last thing Poe ever wrote is a decoration to *Arnheim,* then I'd wager the original story was important to him.

Narrated by an unknown friend, it tells the tale of a man called Ellison who inherits an almost unimaginable quantity of money and, shunning the usual pursuits of the rich to accumulate political power, which he deems trivial with such a fortune, hatches an extraordinary plan in an attempt to spend it. He is obsessed with the idea that the human imagination will always trump the real world when it comes to a natural vista: 'No such paradises are to be found in reality as have glowed on the canvas of Claude.'

As the story develops it becomes clear that Ellison is determined to prove this by finding somewhere that he can improve to the point of perfection. Before he embarks on his unrivalled feat of engineering, he and the narrator tour the world to find the best of nature's landscapes so that he can choose one to perfect. They spend four years experiencing the greatest views nature has contrived to create, until finally they settle on what will become Ellison's canvas. The story then jumps forward, some years after Ellison's death, to a description of the same narrator travelling in a boat along a river to the fabled land. It is the subsequent description of *Arnheim* that takes up most of the story. The landscape is said to be so perfect that there is no stone or leaf out of place. Driving through the oddly perfect scene in Scotland and recalling this story gave me a pleasing – if a somewhat otherworldly – sense of symmetry.

***

By the time we made it to Oban snow was falling heavily. We immediately set off to find out if the ferries were running. It was good news: the town now had power and after a few days of storm-force winds the Sound of Mull was now completely still. We had a few hours to kill but would be on our way that evening. The sun would set on the hour-long journey to the island some seven miles away. We put our bags in the left-luggage racks at the railway station and headed for a pub to eat seafood and drink local beer. Kev was feeling a little more chipper after this, especially as the sun had come out and the snow had stopped, so we set off to see the most obvious of Oban's attractions.

McCaig's Folly is the one thing in the town you can't fail to see. A vast oval of lancet arches, in homage to the Colosseum of Rome, it overlooks the town on a hill immediately behind it. It was built by John Stuart McCaig, a banker who sought to create a lasting monument for his family, while at the same time providing the unemployed local stonemasons with something to do. It was constructed sporadically, but as with most follies the building is merely the bait that forces you to climb a hill and see a view. Despite having come to Mull via Oban for three decades, Kev had never seen the island from up there. The Bay of Oban looks out to the island of Kerrera, but from that vantage point it looks as though it's connected to the mainland some way out of sight to the south. Mull hangs behind it, a range of white-topped mountains banking up and out of the Firth of Lorn.

Interestingly, the word 'firth' has the same origin as the Scandinavian 'fjord', which is something you can tell simply by being near one. You begin to understand where the mythology of the Highlands and Western Islands comes from when you start to inhale the language it preserves in words like 'firth', 'loch' and 'minch', and the new definition it grafts onto others like 'sound' – used here to describe an ocean inlet too wide and too deep to be called simply a bay.

Few visitors understand exactly what these words mean, but we manage to link them up with vague ideas in our heads. Perhaps it's this space or vagueness that gives us the room to dream and the Highlands and Islands their otherworldly quality. At this distance, Mull certainly looked the equal of, if not superior to, any landscape of the imagination.

Kev chuckled, 'Dan, there are at least forty-five breeding pairs of eagles on that island. I wonder whether we'll see a single one.' He patted me on the back and walked away. I stared at the vast peaks, feeling almost overcome, no doubt from lack of sleep and too much alcohol, but thrilled at last to have found a 'Domain of Arnheim' of my own.

***

I recently read a book on neuroscience called *Splendours and Miseries of the Brain* by Semir Zeki. It begins to explain the relationship between the 'ideal' potential Poe sees in man's imagination in contrast with the 'imperfect' mortal reality he is forced to live within.

Zeki explains that the brain uses two different kinds of concepts to make sense of what we experience. One is inherited (like the way the brain deciphers colour) and the other is learned and evolves as we live our lives (like who and what we want to be). Using the perfect house as an example, Zeki explains that our concept for the ideal house is created by our experience of being in or seeing images of hundreds of houses throughout our lives. But because this collage of images and feelings is constantly evolving thanks to our ever-changing experience, the real world can never hope to match this 'perfect' idea we hold in our heads. It's precisely because of the astonishing complexity of the brain – which is the most complicated thing to exist in the known universe, don't forget – that Zeki believes we are destined to a life of suffering. Put simply, our imagination is much better at reflecting our true desires than the real world we live in. It's a compelling, if slightly depressing, logic.

Zeki's book also makes you confront the idea that everything you encounter in your life, whether you consider it to be real or imagined, ultimately resides in thoughts and concepts in your brain. What you see, taste and hear may start out in the real world, but once it's being interpreted in your brain it's completely cut off from reality. This means that the way we interpret the world depends entirely on what our brains are capable of experiencing, implying that the 'real' world is far larger and more complicated than the one we are aware of. Zeki's clash of the concepts that originate in the real world and those of the desires in our imagination echo Poe's point that any vista contrived by nature can always be improved by the artist's vision or, more specifically, the artist's brain.

Zeki then takes on the subject of unrequited love, examining why we seem to find tragic love so compelling, and indeed often more intoxicating than the real thing. Following his logic the answer is that unrequited love sends the imagination off on a reverie of what this supposedly ideal relationship might be by constructing it from the collage of experiences we have felt or seen. This perfect collage of love, then, not being something that can be tested in the real world, becomes even more bewitching than the possibilities of reality. Zeki argues that this is why stories of ill-fated love – from Tristan and Isolde to Romeo and Juliet – are so popular and have been so popular among human beings for millennia: because ultimately they are simply an expression of the way our brains are wired.

He's trying to learn about the workings of the brain, not just by examining neurological processes but also by considering recurring cultural themes that are the collective output of our brains as a species. It's not just love, of course. The idea of human beings struggling to achieve in the real world the perfect image they have of their own lives is something we see all around us. For one thing, it explains why we seem so content to live on the high-velocity conveyor belt of 'tomorrow', because it presupposes happiness in the future as a reward for suffering today. We'll get what we want tomorrow just as long as we get our heads down and do something solid and organised right now – whether it's taking years to get a education so we can have a career, getting a mortgage to buy a house, saving for a family, saving for a pension, all until we retire and finally die, at which point we might be embraced by a concept of religious eternity. We're all planning for tomorrow at the expense of today, because that stops us living in the moment and having to accept the imperfect nature of things as they are.

Nothing exemplifies this approach more than the carrot of the annual holiday that goes with the stick of work. Of course its problem is that by the time we get to tomorrow, as Zeki explains, our life experiences mean what we thought we wanted has changed. We're back to the linear, predictable, planned time of Chronos versus the eternal present of Kairos.

***

A fierce wind funnelled through the Sound of Mull as the ferry chugged across the vast depth of water. The full moon gave us a different kind of illumination as we approached the island and we soon spotted something slightly worrying. Craignure, where we were staying, and the southern half of the island itself were black. Utterly black. They still had no electricity. The storms that I'd forgotten about throbbed back into my head. I fumbled for my phone to ring the pub we'd booked a room in to make sure we would be able to stay. There was still no signal. I remembered the messages and unfamiliar phone numbers I'd ignored earlier and felt a twinge of panic.

Kev and I went downstairs out of the cold and tried

to work out what to do. If the pub had no power it was probably closed and we would have nowhere to sleep. There might not be anyone there at all and we would be completely stranded. Neither of our phones worked. The ferry would return to Oban from Craignure again that night, so we could come back if necessary, but then we risked ruining our chances of seeing eagles the next day. We'd chosen to stay on the southern, less populated section of the island because it was close to the home of a local guide who we'd arranged would pick us up the next morning. It was only 5pm, but the black was so deep and rich as we walked off the ferry that only the moonlight reflecting on the water, and passing car lights, gave us the ability to see.

Happily for us the pub was open – had stayed open, in fact, to see if we would turn up. A handful of locals welcomed us into the warmth of candle and firelight. Bottles of Newcastle Brown Ale and glasses of whisky were dished out between astonished conversations about the weather and much laughter that a wind turbine had blown up because it was too windy. They assumed we would want to stay up in Tobermory and had found us rooms there; the offer of lifts quickly came from some people sitting by the bar, but Kev and I were content to stay where we were. After the journey we'd had, a small inn on a remote Scottish island with only the light of a fire to illuminate the conversations of a community under siege felt like precisely where we were supposed to be. Kev beamed a smile to me at one point and said, 'This slow travel stuff, Dan – is it always like this?' Our hosts seemed surprised at our decision to stay, but we chinked the necks of our beer bottles with each of them in turn, spreading the sense that we were in for some fun.

Outside, the sky was clear and the bright speck of Jupiter offered a reminder of our place in the universe and the mind-blowing nature of celestial time. When you look up into space somewhere as remote as Mull, you can't evade the ephemeral nature of what it means to be alive. If you look up at the stars, or distant suns, across the night sky and remember that the universe contains more of these stars than the planet earth contains individual grains of sand, you can be forgiven for putting your head in your hands and screaming at the baffling absurdity of what it means to 'be'.

It always amazes me that, as a species, we get anything done. These uneasy thoughts were surely more prominent in the minds of our ancestors, living in times when, once the sun had gone, the only light came from flame. Your shoulders hunch slightly when you live in this kind of darkness for any prolonged amount of time. You begin to realise that the seclusion offered by the pools of artificial light you hide in gives you a false sense of control over both the real world and the world of your minds. This sensation of darkness, or the psychological threat you can feel it contains when it envelops you completely, was not only a breeding ground for superstition, creation myths, gods and monsters, though. We may think of ourselves as more developed than the Bronze Age builders of the barrows back on the South Downs, but they still had enough of a connection to the night and to the stars to arrange those barrows to line up with the sun on Midsummer's Day. I wonder whether this connection made them more honest and accepting about their place in the universe, too.

***

Back in the bar the eagles were soon the subject of conversation and our new friends offered advice and varying degrees of pessimism about our chances of finding any. They all talked of the eagles as though they were part of the community. Some 3,000 people live on Mull and a large number of them seem to appreciate what the birds bring to the economy. Everyone had a different idea of places to go to see golden and sea eagles but Alec, the owner of the pub, warned them not to get our hopes up. He was consistently gloomy:

'We have a couple that stay with us for a week every year, he's a photographer so he likes to come off season when there are fewer tourists, well, they left this morning and they didn't see a single one all week.'

He reinforced his pessimism by telling us that now we were here he was closing the pub so he could go home. This was a bit of a surprise at 7pm, but an early night wouldn't do us any harm. The flickering candle flame seemed to tire the eyes like a natural sleeping pill. The news of the eagles was not what we had hoped, but by now we were just thrilled to be there. Alec gave us extra blankets and hopeful promises that the power would soon be back on and all would be well.

We were still without electricity as dawn approached, so Kev and I ate our breakfasts in the bar by the light of the fire. We were excited, but nervous. Grey drizzle fell into the Sound of Mull and soaked our coats as we waited in the early dawn for our guide, Bryan Rains. He arrived in a white minibus a few minutes later, but his warm and friendly demeanour couldn't hide an immediate attempt to lower our expectations.

'We have a very small window of opportunity this morning, a few of hours if we're lucky, but the weather's coming in around lunchtime. You won't see anything after that.'

Determined to be optimistic, I suggested that we'd probably see other wildlife, even if we didn't see eagles.

'Well, the worst way to approach it is to look for something specific – especially eagles – because the things you might otherwise see live in different habitats.'

Refusing to be daunted, I explained the concept of slow travel and how you are usually rewarded with serendipitous delights if you're prepared to take your time. He raised his eyebrows and responded with a simple 'Aye'.

As we headed up the hill, south from Craignure, Bryan explained that there were three places that gave us the best chance of seeing something, so we should head for those straight away. But we were soon waylaid by scenery. Sunrise was around 8.30am and in the twilight we approached what are known locally as Three Lochs. If I thought I'd seen *Arnheim* before, I had no doubt I'd arrived there now. The road was raised slightly at the north end of a valley looking south between two of Mull's smaller mountains, Ben Buie to our right and Creach-Beinn to our left. Apart from the familiar dappled brown of earth, grass and short, crumbling fence poles, the scene was white with snow. Loch Sguabain behind us filled down through 'stepping stones' into the three lochs that fell at eye height off into the distance. The sky was filled with white and grey cloud, rippled with the red light of dawn, and you could see the cut of water grinding down through Gleann a' Chaiginn Mhoir to Lochbuie beyond the hills of the horizon. Kev, who had only visited Mull in summer before, was astonished at the transformation. We all had our binoculars but none of us were thinking about eagles. Sometimes the earth seems to contrive a moment when landscape, light and human emotion perfectly combine.

After a few minutes of contented silence Bryan got out his telescope when Kev thought he'd spotted something. He unfolded the tripod and pulled a small outcrop of Creich-Beinn, 50 yards below the peak, into view. He immediately began to chuckle.

'That's a golden eagle – nice spot, Kev.'

Forgetting myself, I bundled Bryan off the telescope and stared at the dark brown clump of feathers minding its own business on the side of that remote mountainside. Quite content to sit, the eagle turned its head this way and that, showing no inclination to move. Bryan was slightly dismissive and laughed.

'Doesn't count, really – you can barely see it and it's not on the wing!'

But it was good enough for Kev and it was good enough for me. While I gawped through the scope the eagle shook itself, stepped into the air and glided off the ridge and down the other side. It was an instant of natural perfection and far better than anything I could possibly have imagined – precisely because of its reality.

Although I could tell it was a professional requirement, Bryan placed on himself to get us a better sighting than that, now the pressure was off and we could simply enjoy the day. We drew a blank at our next stop, but further up along Glen More we stopped and through Bryan's scope saw two more golden eagles perched on mountain outcrops. I was thrilled, but could tell that until we'd seen something 'on the wing' he would consider it a personal failing. He was scanning the ridges of the mountains around us and I asked him what he was looking for.

'Anomalies, really. If you scan the horizon you're looking for something unusual, even if you're not sure what it is.'

Then he dropped his binoculars, pointed just above the ridge before Cruach Choireadail and called out to Kev, who was looking the other way,

'Two white-tailed sea eagles, on the wing.'

I could see them clearly with the naked eye, but through the binoculars got a sense of the effort required for these enormous birds to fly. The wings were vast.

'Bigger wingspan than your height, can be up to eight feet. Those two are juveniles, though,' Bryan noted.

I'd found monsters at last, but while they soared in my imagination, here the wings were so long that the effort spread through them like a crest moving through a wave. One of them vanished behind the ridge, but the other batted itself down to land and I saw the white tail. It ruffled its feathers and the yellow beak and grey head turned towards me to reveal the grey chest of a juvenile. Even Bryan seemed happy now.

'That's a white-tailed sea eagle. One of the largest eagles you'll see anywhere in the world.'

I turned to him and said, 'What were you going on about? This eagle-watching is a doddle!' And he bent over laughing.

***

In the mountains of Mull it seemed to me that Poe's *Arnheim* is not an expression of the perfection of man's imagination over the nature he finds himself imprisoned within. Ellison's landscape is surely a metaphor for what the contented mind is capable of creating internally, despite the constraints of life and death. Earlier in the story the narrator describes his friend putting his own sense of happiness down to what he calls four conditions of bliss: the health gained from free exercise in the open air, being in love, the contempt of ambition and having an 'object of unceasing pursuit'. The more spiritual this last object is, the greater sense of happiness you will feel.

In the 'pendant' to *Arnheim*, *Landor's Cottage,* we begin to see this more clearly as a traveller stumbles through the bewitching and now familiar landscape to find a simple, but perfect house: 'I could have fancied... that some eminent landscape-painter had built it with a brush.' Inside he finds a couple clearly in love, surrounded by books, artworks and vases of all kinds of fragrant flowers. Poe seems to be telling us that we can control our own image of perfection and escape the tyranny of the real world not living up to what we want it to be. But we achieve this not by trying to conquer the world we live in, but by redesigning the focus of our lives internally, which is surely where *Arnheim* truly resides. For Poe this is achieved by travelling through a landscape, being passionately in love, not falling for the ambition of 'tomorrow' and accepting the lifetime pursuit of expressing your own sense of creativity.

Much as I admire Zeki's work and his attempt to extend the field of neuroscience research from the physical brain out into what the brain is capable of creating, there can be no question that when it comes to travel – as when it comes to love and creativity, for that matter – falling out of control, and beyond the comprehension of your own imagination, is the source of everything. I think this is also what Chatwin is getting at in his most famous quotation when he tells us that: 'Man's real home is not a house, but the Road, and that life itself is a journey to be walked on foot.'

Kev, Bryan and I spent another few hours looking for wildlife on Mull that morning, and Bryan turned out to be right about the weather. But in the early afternoon, over a few celebratory bottles of Newcastle Brown Ale back in Craignure, I got him to concede that I was right about slow travel and the rewards of serendipity. He had no other explanation for the seven different eagles we had gone on to see in just under four hours: four sea eagles (including those two 'on the wing') and three golden eagles. We also saw a mother otter and two cubs swimming along the edge of Loch Scridain, great northern divers, crossbills and countless buzzards, but our most extraordinary sighting came just before the weather forced us to stop for the day. In a location I am not allowed to reveal (but Bryan might take you to if you're lucky) he managed to get a golden eagle sitting in the midst of an oak tree so clearly in his telescope that I could see it blinking. We even got a photo of that one, via his scope and my iPhone, which, despite my prejudice about photographs, is now next to the feather on my office wall at home.

***

Our adventure was not over yet, though. Despite the pub still having no power, a local band arrived to celebrate a friend's 30th birthday. Most of them had grown up in Craignure and rather than being put off by the weather and lack of power, they had seen them as greater incentives to make the journey up from Glasgow. They played long into the night, sitting around a table and communicating with each other by singing and playing music rather than simply talking. Picking up an instrument seemed second nature to them all; they also took it in turns to sing. One girl, wearing an oversized white jumper and yellow wellingtons, successfully pulled off a cover of 'Someone Like You' by Adele. I'd always winced at that song up until then, but she sang it with a vitality that seemed painfully real. Love was communicated through songs all evening. Crispin, the lead singer, seemed so intense I wondered exactly who he was singing, or screaming, to. Then I spotted her between songs, furnishing him with a potent brew of Jack Daniels, Jägermeister and Red Bull. They all drank and sang like demons, licking up love, life and alcohol as a parched tongue might devour dew. At one point a girl demanded to write in my notebook as she fell out of the ladies' toilet. She wrote: 'It's my brother's birthday, Christina.'

While I tried to melt away to write up my notes from the day (travel writers have daily homework), I could see Kev being sucked further and further into the moment. Eventually he made the mistake of idly picking up one of the guitars resting on the wall next to him. The band and their friends all spotted him and Crispin shouted for the whole pub to be quiet. 'You've picked up a guitar, that means you have to play!'

Kev had no escape. They chanted and demanded he sing something for them. By now the entire pub had joined the chorus and at that moment the lights came on. For four days the Craignure Inn and surrounding villages had lived without power and suddenly the darkness was gone. I found myself transported from the warm, dark tavern into an unremarkable pub with tinsel decorations and signed photographs of Bill Bailey on the walls. Everyone laughed, cheered and continued to chant with even more fervour for Kev to play a song. I would have died of embarrassment if I'd been him, but Kev is made of sterner stuff than me. He pulled up a chair, shouted them all to silence and told them he would not sing, but he would tell them a poem. He was seizing the eternal moment in a way I knew he would never forget, and now nothing could stop him. He stared down their jeers with a twinkle.

The pub clearly admired his resolve and urged the 'English' to get on with it. So he did. He stood with chest out and only he knows who he was speaking to and why, but the words tumbled out like the language of the island rising up from forgotten maps coming together in rhyme. God knows how he kept going, but he did. By the time he stopped the entire pub was cheering; Kev was consumed with hugs and more whisky flowed. As he walked away from the single chair that had been his brief stage, the cheering turned into a relentless football terrace-style chant across the entire pub of: 'Poem, poem, one more fucking poem!'

I ducked outside for a sneaky cigarette before heading up to bed and saw Kairos disappearing into the moon-lit night.

Chapter 5

Follow your instincts

To travel hopefully is a better thing than to arrive.
Robert Louis Stevenson

Spending a month in 2007 travelling across Britain in a vintage electric milk float is both the wisest and the craziest thing I've ever done. A few months after we got back I co-wrote a book about the journey called *Three Men In A Float*, but it's only really now, some five years on, that I'm beginning to make sense of what we did.

I made the journey with friends Ian Vince (my co-author) and Prasanth Visweswaran (amateur electrician), and I remember telling people before we left, with tongue not entirely in cheek, that now the planet had been tamed any *real* adventurer would put their ego to one side and spend more time exploring what was under their nose. I convinced myself that we were heading out on a noble quest to discover the 'Real England' and, rather pretentiously – trying to capitalise on some potential eco PR – that we would find out if it was possible to love the planet and travel at the same time.

The truth is that it was all an elaborate joke. There was no great philosophical plan, even though we did get pretty close to our original vision by the time we reached the end. Ian came up with the title in the pub one day and – well, after that, I felt I just had to do it. Even so, we managed to find a milk float only a few weeks before we were due to leave and the first time I drove it on a road was when the lorry deposited it on a cold, windy May evening by the sea in Lowestoft (furthest point east in England). We had set ourselves the task of driving 600 miles to Land's End (furthest point west) in four weeks, but had no idea how we were going to charge the float or where we were going to stay en route. It had a bicycle speedometer wired into the dashboard, no seat belts, incredibly uncomfortable seats and flimsy doors that let in the wind and rain.

I've already mentioned our belated realisation that we would have to rely on complete strangers to recharge the float's battery every night. This dawned on us late at night in Lowestoft and I can still remember the feeling of sheer panic it inspired. Surely we would come unstuck? A month later, exhausted and looking forward to getting home, we lurched to a stop at Land's End. I have no idea how we managed it, but we did. It was all a bit of a blur, to be honest, but of all the odd things I've done over the years it's the one that people most want to talk about.

My first few diary entries after leaving Lowestoft oscillate between exciting new ways of looking at the world that travelling slowly had accessed, worries about lack of money and the constant, haunting threat of disaster because we were so badly prepared. It's one thing to set out to scale Everest and turn back – no one will blame you for that. But embarking on something ridiculous, paradoxically, leaves no room for failure.

The daily organisation and graft the trip required were far more than we'd anticipated. Each morning we were faced with the same problems we'd battled to overcome the day before. Would we do enough miles? Where should we go? Where could we stay? How could we charge this damn milk float? I'm not saying it was unpleasant – we had a fantastic time, it just seems rather ironic in retrospect to have set out on a supposedly slow and relaxing adventure that relied entirely on a ritual of daily struggle.

The float's top speed was 15 miles per hour, so we literally trundled our way across the country. Those first few days the weather was awful and we shivered inside the small and uncomfortable cab, but after a bit of effort we soon found people who were tickled enough by our eccentricity to help as much as they could. By the end of the first week we were beginning to believe the trip was possible and started to relax. That was when our perceptions changed. The quietness of the electric motor meant we didn't scare wildlife, and we got used to being accompanied on small country lanes by hares, rabbits and birds. At one point climbing a hill we were overtaken by a bumblebee.

Our slow pace meant our perception of distance shifted, too. The kind of journey you would think nothing of achieving in two hours in a car took us four exhausting days, which took a lot of getting used to.

When you walk or cycle your mind is occupied and it's physically tiring. A milk float's speed is similar to that of a bicycle, but you're drifting through the countryside in a mobile hammock. After the first week I felt as though we were crossing a vast, unrecorded land as the horizon stretched out before us. It was as if going slowly actually made the country bigger than it had been before.

I thought at the time I was going slightly mad, but when I got home a friend pointed me towards a paper called 'How Long Is the Coast of Britain?', published in 1967 by a mathematician named Benoît Mandlebrot. It suggests that the depth of your journey – in terms of how closely you perceive it – really does increase its length in mathematical terms. The answer to the question posed by the paper is that there is no answer. It's a paradox, because the length of a coastline depends entirely on the way you measure it. It comes down to context, and the context in which you perceive something is a function of the brain.

To explain the coastline paradox you first have to accept that there *is* a definitive geological coastline of Britain, which would depend on high or low tide and all manner of other variables. Assuming you're prepared to accept this, you then have to imagine measuring this coastline with a three-foot ruler. You would, eventually, come up with the coastline's length. But what if you then repeated the experiment with a one-foot ruler? The smaller ruler would give you a greater distance because you would be able to get into lots of nooks and crannies that the three-foot one would have to stretch across.

Now you're probably thinking, 'Well, fine, but if you went down to a one-inch ruler you'd get an even greater distance. At least *that* would be accurate, though, because you can't get smaller than a one-inch ruler.' The problem is, of course, that you can. You can shorten the ruler over and over again, going deeper and deeper, getting smaller and smaller, and the length of the coastline will increase each time. So there really is no definitive answer to the question. It's a rather disconcerting thought, isn't it? We all work on the assumption that the real world is defined according to measurable things, but once you begin to focus on it, the act of measurement itself becomes fraught with uncertainty.

Obviously we weren't travelling at such a tiny scale in our milk float, but we were travelling more 'deeply' than we would have done in our normal lives. We were not measuring this depth as such, but we were viewing it differently in terms of the things we had the time and space to see. We saw no blurred trees from the window of the float, for example, as we would have done from a car. As we passed we saw the outline of each landmark, hedge or tree sharply and clearly. I'm aware that this doesn't entirely make sense, but it does go some way to explaining why we felt so different about the scale of the land we were travelling through.

Following on from this came the realisation that if you spend your life driving around the country on motorways and dual carriageways at great speed you are not really part of the country at all. You have reduced the nation to a journey from A to B and become unconscious of everything in between. Milk floats are not allowed on motorways, so we had to stick to A roads, B roads and, whenever we had the option, little country lanes lined with endless hedgerows. We weren't just aware of the country we were travelling through – we actually became a part of it.

When I say that I felt as if I were part of the landscape as a whole, I don't mean I lost my identity; I mean that I began to see my place in the world I lived in completely differently. There was no divide between what I saw as myself and what I saw as the environment. It was no longer a form of entertainment or something for me to use – we were one and the same thing. Obviously this is very different from how we live our lives normally, when we are removed from the natural world in apparently insignificant ways all the time.

The pace of normal life was revealed to me in brutal terms when my brother-in-law James met up with us while we were staying in a campsite (Pras had by this stage worked out how to extract the amperage the float required from a specific kind of electrical caravan post). We went only a few miles in his car to buy beer and some sausages for a barbecue and he didn't drive particularly quickly – no more than 50 miles an hour – but I felt as if I were trapped in a dragster. I found myself panicking at the absurd speed and the way everything outside the window had suddenly lost its meaning. Physically I felt sick, too. It was then that I realised how unconscious we all are about the speeds we've become accustomed to travelling at.

Another thing being in the car made me realise was how little I *listen* to the country I live in. Like most of us, I am normally in one box or another listening to music or the radio, whether it's a house, pub, car or underground train. Milk floats are very quiet, so we got used to the soundtrack of wherever we happen to be, dappled with the vagaries of conversation. As we were making our journey in the spring we had a constantly reinforcing and enlivening natural soundtrack that we could still hear snatches of behind the white noise of the city. We began to see all kinds of 'modern' noises as interference getting in the way of how things should really be. It was as though the world had regained some of its magic, or I was noticing things that I'd simply got used to ignoring before. By travelling so slowly we had somehow made our perception of the world far less functional, structured and mundane.

In a moment of grandiose profundity I began to wonder whether we were giving the landscape back the sense of mythology that the juggernaut of modernity carelessly thunders through. Of course that *is* mad. What we were doing was changing the context through which our brains experienced our lives. It's precisely this change in perception, or the context the brain uses to make sense of the world, that lies at the heart of what it means to travel.

***

After two weeks we'd got as far as the border between Wiltshire and Dorset and I was beginning to get to grips with our new routine. While one part of my mind wrestled with the interesting new ways of experiencing the world that going slowly helped us to access, the other fought to come up with a more ordered way of dealing with the practicalities. If you drive a milk float to the point where the batteries are depleted completely, they become damaged beyond repair, so we needed a balance. Rather than drive all day and desperately try to find a place to stay and charge each evening, we began stopping in the middle of the day whenever we spotted an industrial estate. We got top-up charges from a Hypnos bed factory (they provide beds for the Queen), from supermarkets and from an electrical warehouse. Not quite as romantic, perhaps, but it gave us much more flexibility in terms of where to spend the night. Being more sensible about how we approached the structure of the trip allowed the new slow way of thinking to offer even more ideas and contrasts with the way we live normally until we'd settled on what seemed like the right balance between the two.

It felt as if we really did change the country as we went through it. Our presence began to change the way the people we met saw the world around them too. Peter, the owner of the bed factory, had an electric forklift somewhere in his vast industrial complex and he said he would have come with us if he hadn't had a wedding in Scotland to go to. A milk-float enthusiast we met in Oxfordshire actually did follow us for a while. Our turning up in a new town or village in a milk float seemed to give people a licence to talk to us in a way they wouldn't usually talk to strangers. We became an event that people converged around, offering them a chance to talk about all sorts of 'crazy' ideas they had always 'dreamed of doing' too. Quite a few people told us how inspiring we were, which was a strange thing to hear when deep down we knew we were acting out an elaborate joke, but it added to the idea that our trip wasn't 'ours' any more.

At the time I saw it as a momentary lifting of the universal veil of cynicism people are usually covered, but now I think that, albeit briefly, we did help them to see their own lives differently. If that sounds far-fetched you'll have to try it yourself. Parties were organised within hours of our approach. People would drive past us in cars, stop, get out and jog alongside us as we trundled down the road, writing down their name, phone number and address in case we went through their town and needed a charge. We started having to *refuse* offers of electricity, free beds for the night and food in the places we stopped. Perhaps travelling slowly releases some kind of contagious way of looking at life that infects the people around you. I have no idea, but there was no question that something tangible had started to happen.

We continued into Devon and Cornwall, alternating between the homes of strangers, campsites and the odd luxury hotel. By now our self-confidence was unassailable and we were marching up to people and demanding their help. Not in a rude way – we had just begun to realise that when someone gave us a charge we were not the only ones receiving a gift. That sounds arrogant but it's not meant to. I lost count of the number of conversations we had with people who seemed happy to reveal their innermost feelings and secrets about their hopes and ideas. I felt as if we'd tapped into a whole new way of living that was a mirror for other people's dreams.

In retrospect, the push and pull of the practicalities and inspiration of our milk-float trip and the way it seemed to excite people are the perfect illustrations of the conflict inherent in how the brain operates – a struggle between order on the one hand and being open to the unknown on the other. The concept of the divided brain that was put forward in the 1960s and '70s argued that one half of the brain delivered reason and the other emotion. It has now been established that this is not true – both sides contribute to each aspect of our experience in different ways. There is no question that the brain is divided, though. The hemispheres are joined at the base by something called the corpus callosum, which facilitates connections between the two. Neuroscientists now believe that one of the functions of the corpus callosum is actually to *inhibit* the connections between the two hemispheres, which implies there is a battle going on (more on this later). At the front of the human brain you'll find the frontal lobes, the part of the brain responsible for conscious thought. These lobes allow us to stand back from the immediacy of experience, to think and plan ahead. They are where empathy and responsibility come from.

***

In an attempt to find a less abstract explanation for the way my views on the world changed on our milk-float trip – and in slow travel generally – I turned to a book called *Incognito* by the acclaimed neuroscientist David Eagleman. If you were under the impression that your consciousness ultimately drives your behaviour, you'd be wrong. In the last few decades neuroscientists have discovered something rather unsettling about how conscious we really are. Eagleman reveals various experiments that prove our unconscious brain is in control of most of what we do. In one study he cites men who were given a selection of images of women's faces and asked to rate them for attractiveness. One half of the images showed women with dilated pupils, the other undilated. The men consistently rated the images of women with dilated pupils as being more attractive, even though none of them offered that as an explanation for their choice. They were making a decision, but had no idea what their brains were basing it on.

A few years earlier I'd read a study by a team of scientists at the Max Planck Institute for Human Cognitive and Brain Sciences that sought to understand how the brain makes decisions. They asked people to perform the very simple task of pressing a button with either their left or their right hand while their brain signals were being monitored. The subjects of the test could decide which hand to use whenever they liked, but they had to say as soon as they had made up their mind. Unusually in a test of this kind, the researchers were interested in what happened in the brain *before* a conscious decision was made. The astonishing result was that by analysing signals from the brain the researchers could predict which hand the subject would use to press the button *seven seconds* before the subject 'knew' it themselves. When it comes to simple tasks like this our unconscious mind is clearly in control.

This experiment, along with the ones Eagleman describes, has all sorts of implications about the concept of free will, but the Max Planck researchers pointed out that, while their experiments seemed to prove that our unconscious mind made decisions without the conscious mind being aware of them, they did not discover whether or not the conscious mind had the ability to overrule the decisions of the unconscious once they had been made.

What is clear is that our unconscious mind makes decisions for us all the time. Eagleman uses the analogy of a newspaper that condenses the news into the most important and interesting stories. It can't contain *all* the news in the world, so it presents you with a selection so that you have a reasonable understanding of what's going on. Your consciousness is the newspaper your unconscious has created in order to give you the highlights of its activities, rather than letting you know every single thing it's doing on your behalf. In the same way, every time you think you've had an idea you'll find your unconscious has actually been whirring away at it for some time; it only presents the thought to your conscious brain when it's ready, at which point you stop and think, 'Wow, I've just had a great idea.'

I found that particularly fascinating because I've always been a firm believer that you don't have ideas, ideas have you. They descend in the unlikeliest of places, while you're in the bath, when you're drifting off to sleep or staring out the window. You can't force them, they just happen. But apparently we do have ideas after all – as long as you can accept that your unconscious mind, as well as your conscious one, is 'you'.

Another analogy neuroscientists often use is that our unconscious is like our autopilot mode, while the conscious mind comes into action when 'we' take over the controls. While typing these words on my keyboard, I am completely unconscious of the processes my mind, eyes, arms and hands have to go through to make sure I hit the correct keys in the right order. If I performed all these actions consciously, it would take me years to write a book like this. Thankfully, over the years, my brain has become very efficient when it comes to typing, so it doesn't need to bother my conscious mind with what it's doing behind the scenes.

But if the unconscious mind is so busy making all these decisions and helping us function in ways we're not consciously aware of (like walking or breathing), what does the conscious mind actually do, and is it really the place you'll find what you think of as 'you'? To explain this, Eagleman takes you back to when you first learned to drive a car. At first you are conscious of everything you're doing because it's all so new and you begin to wonder if you will ever train yourself to do it intuitively. A few years after you've passed your test you find that you have. This is how consciousness works. It's activated to deal with new or extraordinary things as they occur in your daily life. If the door of a parked car opens into the lane you are driving in, or if a child jumps out into the road, then you move from the unconscious to the conscious mind and all of a sudden you become aware of what you're doing. Studies into brain behaviour when people play computer games have shown that when we are faced with a new task or game the brain works incredibly hard to try to deal with it. Once it has made the new neurological connections – has worked out the right procedure to deal with each task – the unconscious mind takes over and everything becomes much more efficient. So we become less and less conscious of how we do things that we already know how to do. This is how we learn, evolve and take control of our environment, whether it's learning to play the guitar, finding our way around where we live or knowing the most efficient way to find food. If we're faced with familiar situations our unconscious mind is in charge; once we're out of its comfort zone the conscious mind takes over.

***

This all has very interesting implications when it comes to travel. It suggests that when travel takes us out of a predictable routine we do become more aware, because our conscious mind has been activated to deal with the new things we're experiencing. This could explain why travel feels so vibrant and exciting. Looking back, this idea offers a tantalising explanation for some of my own slow travel experiences. Could the sudden, heightened sense of excitement and control at that crossroads in France when Henry and I ran out of water have been my conscious mind taking control? Was the moment of repulsion in that hotel bar in Warsaw a sign that my conscious mind had recognised a familiar situation and was handing back control to the unconscious one? Does the same thing explain the heightened sense of travelling alone, as opposed to the comfort zone of familiar, polite conversation when you travel with someone you know?

This could also account for the different ways in which we perceive time. We all know the unconscious mind deals with time differently. How often have you driven a car along a familiar journey, the route to work or to see your parents, and been amazed at how quickly you arrived? It's almost as if you zoned out and didn't notice time passing the way it normally does. Compare that to the slower sensation you experience when you are driving somewhere new. That first, unfamiliar journey always seems to take far longer than the same journey taking you back home – could this be related to our conscious and unconscious mind too? What about the times when I've been out hunting with falcons and I've felt as though I had begun to adopt the hawk's perceptions, spotting mice and voles darting through the grass beneath my feet? Was that my conscious mind having to elbow the unconscious, predictable routine of my normal perceptions out of the way because I was forced to live *in the moment* and see the world the way hawks and falcons do?

This could also explain why people seem to 'find themselves' when they are travelling, because they are more conscious of the experience of being alive when they are journeying in new and exciting ways. Being in alien places and cultures will inevitably result in an increased connection with yourself, because it's in these new situations that your consciousness wakes up. You've turned off the unconscious autopilot that runs your normal life and started to take conscious control. Of course there's less need to bother your conscious mind if you deliberately travel in a way that is familiar, safe and routine.

Rather deliciously, this offers up a way of understanding – and actually defining for once – the difference between travel and a holiday. Sometimes we want the relaxation of a holiday, precisely because we won't feel overly challenged, and so on holiday our unconscious mind remains in control. On other occasions we want travel that will push ourselves into experiencing different ways of looking at the world, which brings our conscious mind to the fore. This is not to claim that there is a right or wrong way to travel, or that you can't find a combination of the two – perhaps that really is the Holy Grail; simply that there is a neurological way of differentiating between the two experiences. As a father of two young children, I sometimes find that an unconscious holiday where everything is predictable and easy is precisely what I'm looking for, but most of the time I want to travel and let my conscious mind take control.

***

There's no doubt in my mind that travel has the capacity to alter your view of the world. Discovering that this echoes the way my brain works feels very logical, because I'm certainly more conscious of the experience of my life as a result of having less control. The notion that travel and exposure to different cultures could have a tangible effect on the brain's perception of the world reminded me of a man called Rupert Isaacson I met a year ago.

Isaacson is an incredibly inspiring and exciting person to be around. A British-born travel writer himself who now lives in Texas, he embarked on the kind of once-in-a-lifetime journey you read books and watch films about but never get around to doing yourself. Not only did he do it, but he wrote a book and made a film of the experience called *The Horse Boy.* They tell the story of his journey on horseback across Mongolia with his wife Kristin and four-year-old son Rowan in an attempt to heal, rather than cure, Rowan's autism. The difference between the goal of healing and curing tells you a lot about the Isaacsons.

In *The Horse Boy* Isaacson describes in harrowing terms how he and Kristin fought to deal with their son's condition as Rowan approached his second birthday:

> Life had suddenly become a mechanical drudgery of driving from one therapy to another and dealing with insurance companies, therapists and Rowan's ever-mounting, inexplicable tantrums. Tantrums on the street...as Rowan, a tiny human decibel machine, hurled himself to the ground and began to bang his head so hard against the concrete we had to restrain him, head and heels thudding into the hard paving as if he were an epileptic. Sometimes his rages would

be accompanied by projectile vomiting, like that of the child in *The Exorcist*.

Online research led to conflicting advice about how to cope, but it yielded information that helped the two baffled parents begin to understand Rowan's traumatic experience of the world. Autistic children have far more nerve cells in their brains than 'neuro-typical' people, so their lives are assaulted by a kind of sensory overload we can barely imagine. Rowan was eventually diagnosed with something called PDD – 'persuasive development disorder not otherwise specified' – that turned out to mean a condition similar to autism that no one really understood. It was thought to be caused by a reaction between genes and the environment, which led to a theory that because it was biological in nature it could be treated biologically too. So the Isaacsons started feeding their son a cocktail of pills that he would drink only if they were mixed with the mania-inducing sugar rush of chocolate milk. Despite this, and a plethora of different treatments and approaches, nothing seemed to have much effect. Rowan was increasingly lost in his own world, speaking very little and when he did only echoing words that he heard from other people or on the TV.

But Rupert and Kristin soon found a form of treatment that their son did love – running wild in the woods at the back of their house. Rowan also appeared to have a connection with animals. Not only did he respond to images of animals, they seemed naturally to get along with him: they let him play with them and physically manipulate them in ways they would normally resist from other people. In what turned out to be a breakthrough, one day Rowan ran off onto a neighbour's land and into a field of five horses. Despite being a passionate horseman and horse trainer himself, Isaacson had deliberately kept Rowan away from larger animals because of the danger they could put him in. Terrified, he relates what happened next:

> ...he threw himself on to the ground, belly-up, right in front of the alpha mare, the herd leader, a big bay quarterhorse called Betsy. I froze. Any sudden movement – his or mine – could spook her and leave him trampled and broken on the ground. I knew this mare. She was quiet to ride but was famously grumpy towards the other horses, over whom she was the unquestioned boss...She stood stock still, as did the other four horses...unsure whether or not to be alarmed by this strange little human wriggling at her feet. Then she dipped her head to Rowan's soft, writhing form and mouthed with her lips. The sign of equine submission.

Despite his years of experience with horses, Isaacson had never seen this happen. When he laid Rowan on Betsy's back a few moments later the boy became serenely calm and started to talk in ways he had never done before.

The second piece of inspiration that would lead to the family's epic journey fell into place a few weeks later. Isaacson had previously spent years living with the Bushmen of the Kalahari, the latest in a line of Africa's hunter-gatherers that has been traced back 80,000 years. He had personal experience of the Bushmen's ability to heal people and had helped raise the money for a tour across America to publicise their fight against the Botswana government at the UN. Now the Bushmen were coming to America to meet with other healers, tribal leaders and shamans from all over the world to get advice on how they had fought for their land rights, and the Isaacsons were going to be there too.

When the family arrived at the gathering in the Big Bear Mountains east of Los Angeles, Rowan behaved as you might expect, charging around, causing chaos and upsetting a few people. Then a healer from Zimbabwe called Mandaza told Isaacson that Rowan was 'one of us' and asked if he could sit with him. Mandaza began to run his hands over Rowan's head and down his spine. Isaacson expected his son to 'freak out', as he usually did when someone he didn't know tried to touch him, but Rowan became completely calm and started to giggle. Later that day as they walked through the woods he began to talk unprompted for the first time. Over the next few days he started to play with other toddlers in a way he had never done before. Once the family got back home, however, he reverted to his 'normal' self.

It was at this point that Isaacson began researching the two things that seemed to have the most positive impact on Rowan's life: shamanic healing and horses. Mongolia turned out to be the place where horses first evolved during the ice age, and where shamans originally came from too; indeed Shamanism and Buddhism were the state religions. The most powerful shamans were said to live among the Reindeer people in the northernmost fringes of Mongolia. It took a bit of persuading, not to mention work to find enough money to fund the trip, but eventually Kristin consented and they found themselves accompanied by a small film crew boarding an Aeroflot flight to the Mongolian steppe. Kristin joked that, if the shamans could get Rowan toilet trained, however insane the trip turned out to be, it would be worth it.

Autism is a highly complex neural condition that effects the way people communicate and interact with the world. Autistic children's brains initially seem to develop much more quickly than those of other children, but the growth rate slows as they get older. This could account for certain overdeveloped abilities autistic people have in specific areas, while other areas of their experience remain underdeveloped. Rowan's apparent connection with animals led his father to visit Dr Temple Grandin, an autist herself who has, in her own words, gone from being almost unreachable as a child, 'rocking in a chair and eating wallpaper', to becoming an academic at Colorado State University, best-selling author and subject of a Hollywood movie starring Claire Danes. She explained that many autists like her think in images rather than language. Animals, clearly, don't use language either. They are sensory thinkers, thinking in sounds, smells and images, which explains why they are able to extract so much information from the world that we are oblivious to. Thinking in images is a logical explanation of why Rowan used images of animals to communicate his own feelings, and how he was able to 'understand' animals in a way 'neuro-typical' people couldn't.

You'll find lots of Dr Grandin's talks online. I watched one in which she explains how important it is to be open to different ways of thinking. She splits the way people think into three categories – visual, using patterns and verbal. Although most people use a combination of all three, she argues that autistic people tend to be more extreme in how they think in one of these three areas. Her own thought processes are formed by hypersensitive image recall, as though her mind were sifting through the results of a Google image search. She also suggests that it's the extremes of each way of thinking you'll find in autistic people that actually account for the evolution of our species. In her words: 'If by some magic autism had been eradicated from the face of the earth, then men would still be socialising in front of a wood fire at the entrance to a cave.' If that sounds far-fetched, consider how successful technical innovation would be today if you removed all those on the autistic spectrum from Oxford and Cambridge Universities or Silicon Valley.

***

When the Isaacsons arrived in Mongolia their guide, Tulga, met them off the plane and a few days later took them to the place where the first healing had been arranged. It would be the largest gathering of shamans since the fall of Communism, the Soviets having banned the ancient practice to the point that even owning a drum had been enough to get you sent to prison – it was only now beginning to return. Some of the shamans had travelled hundreds of miles to take part. That day the Isaacson family was put through an extraordinary trial of patience and pain – both Rupert and Kristin were whipped repeatedly as the ritual reached a peak of dancing and noise. They were ushered from one shaman to another in a line and asked to perform a bizarre sequence of actions. Oddly, considering his normal response to intense stimulation, Rowan endured it with less complaint than many of the treatments he'd suffered back at home. He seemed to find it all rather funny. Despite the apparent mania of the situation, drums being banged and shamans in a trance shrieking in his face, he kept laughing and at one point tried to pull a shaman's mask off. Then he did an incredibly loud fart and began shouting, 'Farty noise! More shamans!'

By the time they'd made it through three hours of this process, one of the shamans told Isaacson that if they went through this procedure once a year for three years Rowan would be healed completely, but there was still one final ritual to come. This one was difficult to read, because it involved Rowan being hit on the back. He screamed and Isaacson jumped in to stop it, but he was pulled away and then the ritual ended. Another shaman took a clearly distraught Rowan into her arms and started to sing. Immediately he calmed down and called her his Mongolian mother.

It's hard to know what to make of these scenes. From the comfort of your sofa it looks insane, but the book conveys a bewitching sense of immersion that the film can't quite communicate – at least to a predominantly verbal thinker like me. Isaacson constantly questions his own motives and pushes himself to answer for his own sense of desperation, but even so, you can tell part of him really does believe in the process. He repeatedly describes the reason for putting everyone through it as a 'hunch' or as following his 'inner voice', even though he can't verbalise exactly what the hunch or voices mean.

The tagline of the film is 'How far would you travel to heal someone you love?', which might seem sentimental to anyone who doesn't have children. The rest of us can't help but admire the mix of courage and self-belief. It's exhausting just reading about it, and the journey on horseback hasn't even started yet. A few days later, Tulga leads the family to find the group of nomads who will take them on the eight-day ride to the sacred Lake Sharga and then on to find the Reindeer people. When the family finally arrive at the nomads' camp, having driven across tiny dirt tracks into, quite literally, the middle of nowhere, Isaacson describes how he feels his perceptions change. What we've learned about how the conscious and unconscious parts of the brain deal with new experiences gives us an insight into what's going on in his mind:

> These kinds of arrivals from nowhere into nowhere – they reset the brain, like pressing the button on

your internal odometer so that it reads three zeroes once again, or wiping a blackboard clean. *What now?* Your brain asks. *What now?*

By this stage Rowan and Tulga's son Tomoo were behaving like any other young boys – playing together, laughing and joking. Only they were doing it among the nomads' animals beneath a Mongolian mountain range. Isaacson didn't dare believe the shamans' rituals were working, but Rowan had never before played with other children in the way he was with Tomoo. When they woke in the morning they would begin their ride.

There isn't room here to detail the rest of their journey, but Rupert's personality and the obvious love he and Kristen have for their son are an inspiration for any parents who think they have it tough. Most importantly for our purposes, it resulted in a definite change in Rowan – a change that remained long after they got home. Today Rowan has a much higher quality of life than he had before. He has not been 'cured' of his autism, but there is no doubt in his parents' and friends' minds that he is a different child. Who knows whether it was due to the shamanic healing? Perhaps travelling together as a family became an act of healing, or simply riding horses? The fact is that the courage – or hunch – that set them on such a journey somehow altered the way Rowan's brain was able to make sense of his world. The Isaacsons' story surely proves we are all capable of accessing a different part of our minds when we travel, even if not always to the same degree.

***

My milk-float trip across Britain seems rather weak in comparison to the story of *The Horse Boy*, but both journeys relied on the same three principles. Both followed a hunch that it was the right thing to do, both involved travelling slowly and both relied on the generosity of communities that neither party had visited before. And we mustn't fall into the trap of feeling inadequate about our own travel experiences when comparing them to apparently more noble ones. All experiences are meaningful if we embark on them authentically and if we are honest with ourselves.

The sense of community we found on our journey across Britain is the part I now remember most keenly. I've never been fond of 'sights', so we did our best to avoid any obvious ones we were near. What we did find was a different kind of sight. Ones that moved around in an unpredictable way, so that you couldn't plan a trip on the assumption of seeing them. We discovered them not from a guidebook or brochure, but from following our own instincts and sense of curiosity. They were sitting on bar stools, lounging by roaring fires, up a tree, peering underneath the chassis of the float to check our brake cables, working in factories, living by the side of the road, in campsites; we even found one in a massive supermarket. These were sights with their own stories, philosophies and ideas. Of course they were people, not places or things. People we met because we did what we did. We were lucky that our lives intersected with theirs.

Those experiences were unrepeatable, unpredictable and unbeatable; it's those moments, conversations and jokes that I remember five years later. In the future I'm sure I'll remember other moments and other ideas from that trip, because travel is an evolving experience. It doesn't take place in photographs or your past, having been scythed down by the pace of Chronos. Instead, it's tucked up there in your memory and when you need a bit of it, or a new perspective on something hidden within it, it will emerge into your conscious mind.

***

Rupert Isaacson's journey didn't end when he got home either. He took what he had learned through his experience of helping Rowan and set up a charity called The Horse Boy Foundation. He now offers horse therapy for people across the autism spectrum. Through their love for their son and sheer force of will, he and Kristin stumbled on a genuine treatment that offers hope to many other families, because it turns out that being on a horse *can* alter the brain's perception of the world. Constantly having to adjust your physical position to keep your balance (as you do when riding a horse) is now known to activate the part of the brain that's activated during learning. Combining that with the sense of security a child feels when being held by an adult sitting on the horse behind them, and the fact that, while they are riding, the adult can reassure the child verbally without forcing him or her into making eye contact (which can be unsettling for autists), all seems to contribute to helping some autistic children come out of themselves. It's also been proven that riding horses releases oxytocin in the brain, which makes you feel calm and secure.

Isaacson's hunch and inner voice about a horseback journey across the Mongolian steppe in search of shamans suddenly begins to make sense in a scientific context, even though on the face of it it was as unscientific as it could possibly be. At which point his hunch and inner voice telling him he was heading on the right path become rather intriguing, don't they? What made him decide such an epic journey was the right thing to do?

Chapter 6

Lose your mind

The intuitive mind is a sacred gift and the rational mind is a faithful servant. We have created a society that honours the servant and has forgotten the gift.
Attributed to Albert Einstein

If following a seemingly insane hunch into the unknown is one way to approach travel, the opposite must be to go in search of things that you know are already there. On my way to work in London I often walk past Buckingham Palace, through Green Park and along to Piccadilly Circus before heading up into Soho. Buckingham Palace is always busy with tourists and over the years I've begun to notice something strange about the people who descend in such numbers to stand and stare through the railings.

As the tourists walk towards the palace they are filled with excitement and conversation, but that seems to end in front of the building itself. Even the giggling schoolchildren wearing identical rucksacks, draping their arms over each other like rows of table-football players, seem to fall into a kind of trance. You get the inevitable routine of posing for photographs, but beyond that you'll notice people looking off into the middle distance in a state of apparent confusion. The road is usually blocked off, so they spill out towards the fountain, drifting around in circles as though in search of something that didn't turn out to be there.

You are unlikely to notice this vacant look when you're a tourist yourself, but it becomes very obvious when it happens in a place you know well. I too have assumed this baffled expression on countless occasions. I remember going to the pyramids in Egypt when I was 15 and being briefly amazed; but boredom set in very quickly. I stood there thinking, 'How long am I supposed to look at them?' and 'What am I looking for?' As we left in the coach a few hours later I felt a terrible sense of emptiness and put this down to the fact that although I had seen them I hadn't actually touched them. I still recall my despair at not having had a proper experience and I vowed to return.

I haven't been back since, but in retrospect I now wonder whether touching them would have made any difference. That feeling of not having found what I'm looking for is something I've felt many times since. If anything, seeing a 'must see' for myself tends to *reduce* the amazement and intrigue I felt for it before. Sometimes it has a brief shock value, because it's so immense, but I usually find my mind slips into a state of emptiness as the throng of tourists I have become part of consumes me and we file along in an orderly queue. I've wandered aimlessly, but not in a good way, around quite a few of the world's most famous sights and always found the experience oddly hollow. I've trudged around churches, museums and galleries – so many I can barely distinguish one from the other – but I do recall that aching feeling of 'tourist legs' each time. I'm beginning to wonder if we're all colluding in a conspiracy of silence. Does anyone find this practice remotely enriching?

There are other tell-tale signs of 'must sees'. You know you're close to one of London's most famous sights, for example, if you find decent public loos. This hints at the priorities that governments place on the tourist's experience of a city at the expense of the locals, but let's not go into that here. The atmosphere around these places is the same the world over – too often they feel completely unauthentic, which is proven by the fact that local people avoid them as much as they can. St James's Park near Buckingham Palace is a case in point. Londoners never go there. It's full of tourists buying hot dogs and flag emblazoned T shirts and hats. Places like this become symbols of a nation but they are entirely false, existing only in the minds of the tourists and reinforcing what they were expecting to find. Interestingly, these sights are usually historic, representing the past, not the present. They rarely reflect the ideas, values or ways of thinking that each culture contains at the moment when you visit. But the historical, cultural or geographical familiarity offers a strange kind of sanctuary all the same.

Of course it's all very well people like me, Zweig and the other travel writers I've mentioned saying this, but what's really fascinating is why so many of us are content to experience travel in this way. I'm not claiming – in the words of Evelyn Waugh – that 'the tourist is the other fellow', because I'm no different from anyone else. But for some reason when we travel like this we *want* our preconceptions to be confirmed. Tourists *want* a photograph of a London bus, a red telephone box and Buckingham Palace, because seeing these things proves that they have been there. Often taking a photograph is enough and after that we're happy to head off somewhere else. But we haven't actually travelled any further than our own preconceived idea.

So *why* are these clichés so comforting? Why do we all herd ourselves around between these empty destinations? Why do I have a photograph of myself on the Eiffel Tower, the Charles Bridge in Prague, the Spanish Steps in Rome, St Mark's Square in Venice, the World Trade Center in New York? I could go on and on. We all could. But what are we really looking for?

It's not just visiting the obvious sights that reinforces a sense of order when we travel. The language we use when describing the process is interesting too. People say, 'Have you *done* the such and such?' 'Oh yes, I *did* that years ago.' As though the act of physically spending a few hours somewhere is all that's necessary to understand it entirely. Why do we refer to our travel experiences with this overriding sense of conquest and finality? If you come to London you have to 'do' Buckingham Palace, in the same way you 'do' the Colosseum if you're in Rome. Once you've 'done' somewhere there is no need to do it again. Then there's the way people talk about travel itself. If you mention a plan to go to Vietnam one evening in a pub it won't be long before someone pipes up with 'Oh, I've been there' with disdain in their voice, planting their flag into the virgin territory of your conversation as though they were cut from the same cloth as Columbus himself. We want to feel we've achieved something when we travel, but the structure we impose seems to make that impossible. The desire for order is obviously available in what the tour operators offer with their all-inclusive holidays and package deals, but even if we don't travel under their umbrella, most of us herd ourselves through an itinerary that includes the predictable sights just the same.

***

I believe it is a combination of these desires that ultimately explains the paradox of modern travel. We have turned it into the opposite of what we intuitively understand it to be. We seek to experience the exotic and the unknown through the perspective of order and familiarity. It's tempting to conclude that this need for reliability and order makes us travel in the 'wrong' way, while my intuitive sense that I had to travel across England in a milk float, as well as the hunch that sent the Isaacson family across Mongolia on horseback, are examples of travelling in the 'right' way. But neither of these is actually 'right' or 'wrong'. Most people are no more likely to drive across Britain in a vintage milk float than I am to go to the Buddha Beach Bar in Marbella. To my mind, we all want a combination of *both* experiences, but too much of the travel infrastructure we're offered is designed around ease and reliability and very few of us are prepared to embrace the intoxication of travelling into the complete unknown. What we need is something in between, or at least an understanding that both are available, so that we can consciously decide between the two. It's as if our brains – in terms of the way we experience the world – are fundamentally unbalanced, and as a result we're rarely able to find what we're looking for.

We saw earlier how we access our consciousness in different ways, but the brain is much more complicated and deeper than the difference between our conscious and unconscious mind. At this point my quest for information about the brain resulted in my discovering the work of the psychiatrist, philosopher and author Iain McGilchrist, in the form of his book *The Master and his Emissary*. Like Zeki, McGilchrist is as interested in the output of the brain, in terms of how and why we live the way we do, as he is in its intricate workings, and he focuses his vast intellect on drawing links between the two. The title of his book hints at what he sees as the battle being played out between the two hemispheres of the brain. One side, he argues, seems to be winning, which is why the way we see the world is becoming increasingly skewed to that point of view.

McGilchrist borrows the analogy of the Master and the Slave from Nietzsche, and refocuses it as a conflict between the Master and his Emissary. The Master is described as a spiritual leader whose wisdom enables his subjects to lead happy and fulfilling lives. In order to retain his sense of perspective he must stand back from his people's day-to-day concerns and use a series of Emissaries to act on his behalf. One of them becomes so efficient that the Master comes to rely on him completely. In due course, the Emissary begins to question what it is the Master actually does. He becomes more and more enraged because he is the one doing all the work. Eventually, he deposes the Master and only then discovers what he was up to. With the Emissary unable to replicate his Master's wise counsel, the society soon falls into collapse.

For McGilchrist, the Master represents the right hemisphere of the brain and the Emissary the left. The right hemisphere is more intuitive and open to the unknown, while the left relies on structure and order and reinforces its own belief in what it already knows. The left hemisphere gives the world order through the use of language. The right hemisphere, on the other hand, has a much more abstract role. The key, McGilchrist believes, is to achieve a balance between each hemisphere's perceptions of the world but, he argues, in the West we have become accustomed to allowing the Emissary – the left hemisphere's preference for order and narrow focus – to take control.

It's important to stress that he's not claiming that the brain is divided in the way people thought in the 1960s and '70s. What he is saying is that after that theory was found to be untrue, we began to ignore the very clear differences between the hemispheres of the brain. His work is an attempt to make us revisit the obvious differences and try to make sense of them. He also constantly reiterates that both hemispheres are required to perform most of the functions we will touch upon here, but often (as in the case of language) they do predominantly take place in one side of the brain.

McGilchrist makes his case on the basis of what we know about the way each hemisphere functions and the fact that the division of the brain has become more pronounced through evolution – human brains are becoming more divided, not less. The *corpus callosum*, which I mentioned earlier and which is now known to inhibit the communication between the two hemispheres, has also grown larger through evolution. From this it's clear that, as a species, we're destined to have increasingly divided brains as we continue to evolve.

Birds and mammals also have divided brains, and McGilchrist gives the example of a bird eating seed on a gritted path to explain the differences in the way the two hemispheres work. The bird has to be able to focus on picking up the seed, as opposed to the similar-sized grit, but at the same time it has to protect itself by being aware of the possibility of predators and to look out for potential mates nearby. McGilchrist explains that birds use the left hemisphere of their brains to focus attention on the seed and the right hemisphere to be open to the unknown. In the human brain, the right hemisphere is also active in a more alert, sustained and open way, while the left has a much narrower focus and sharper attention to detail. The left hemisphere controls the right side of the body and the right hemisphere controls the left.

McGilchrist gives examples of patients who lose the use of the right hemisphere through an accident or a stroke; in some extreme cases the patient will deny the existence of the left-hand side of the body entirely. He cites a woman who refused to accept that her left arm was hers, even though her working eye could see that it was connected to her body. Because the two halves of the brain had been disconnected by damage to the right hemisphere, the left hemisphere couldn't cope with a broader, more intuitive experience of the world: without the right hemisphere to communicate with it relies entirely on what it already knew, which is that it 'was' the right side of the body, not the left. So it was forced to conclude that what it could see was not real. This tells us that a balanced view of the world, and a rational one for that matter, require both hemispheres, even though you can still live a relatively normal life if you are unfortunate enough to 'lose' the use of one half of your brain completely.

What makes these different perceptions so fascinating, according to McGilchrist, is the way the frontal lobes allow us to stand back from our immediate experience. It's this distance – enabled by the conscious mind and combined with each hemisphere's view of the world – that allows us to manipulate and impose order on the world and to empathise with it and other living things we encounter. In one of his talks McGilchrist condenses his immense book into a list of the actions each half of the brain performs that result in their different ways of perceiving the world. He prefaces this by reiterating that reason and imagination take place in both hemispheres, but the list gives his ideas a more structured – dare I say it, left-hemisphere – approach.

> The world of the left hemisphere is dependent on denotative language and abstraction, [it] yields clarity, and the power to manipulate things that are known, fixed, static, isolated, de-contextualised, explicit and general in nature but ultimately lifeless.
>
> The right hemisphere by contrast yields a world of individual, changing, evolving, inter-connected, implicit, incarnate living beings within the context of the lived world. But [it is] never fully graspable and never perfectly known.

McGilchrist describes the left hemisphere as the Silvio Berlusconi of the brain: it controls the media of language, and this accounts for the imbalance in our perceptions, because the right hemisphere requires the left to voice its ideas and concerns. I don't know about you, but I often have inklings of ideas, or intuitive thoughts that I can't quite put into words. It goes back to what I said earlier about needing language to help us form and verbalise our ideas. The right hemisphere of our brains is full of concepts and ways of seeing things, but it relies on our language to express them.

This gives us a deeper understanding of the paradox behind what we want when we travel. The left hemisphere of the brain understands things that are reliable, familiar and narrow in focus, which is probably why we are keen to go out and buy a guidebook as soon as we've decided on our destination. But the right brain wants us to be open to new ideas and new ways of looking at things, which could be why we quickly get bored with the information the guidebook contains. Modern travel is sold to us on the basis of what the right hemisphere of the brain tells us intuitively travel is all about – exploration, learning, the unknown – but the process of travel itself increasingly conforms to the left hemisphere's structured view of the world.

Our most enjoyable travel experiences surely offer a combination of the two approaches, a balance between order and the unknown. My slow travel adventures offer examples of this. Inconvenient as it may be to take long-distance trains instead of aeroplanes, those trains are (for the most part) predictable in terms of the time they take and the place you ultimately want to go – which pleases the left hemisphere of the brain. But there is still a large element of the unknown for the combination of my conscious mind and my right hemisphere to revel in, because I'm confronted with new languages, cultures, people, things outside the window and slow ideas along the way.

***

So if the conventional package deal and the sight-seeing holiday is the left hemisphere's kind of travel and slow travel is a more balanced approach, what kind of travel would be accessed by the right hemisphere? For an example of this, I'd like to introduce you to Jay Griffiths and her book *Wild*.

I've read *Wild* many times, but doing so after encountering McGilchrist's ideas made it even more alluring. The best travel books aren't simply descriptions of places – they're travelogues of the writer's mind, too. Griffiths' book begins with an account of a terrible bout of depression and her decision to attempt to cure it by going in search of a hallucinogenic drink called *ayahuasca* created by shamans in the Amazon jungle. She acknowledges that this is a rather extreme way of dealing with the problem, but she is so debilitated by depression that it seems the last of very few remaining options. This decision could be construed, rather like Isaacson's hunch, to be the left hemisphere of the brain handing over to the right hemisphere, having exhausted all the apparently reliable and predictable methods of getting the situation under control.

Griffiths uses the metaphor of a wasteland of the mind to explain her depression and seeks its physical and mental opposite by going in search of something wild. When she drinks *ayahuasca* with a shaman in the jungle she describes it as like 'drinking hemlock and the stars'; she experiences visions and suffers violent physical purges. We all remain wild, she reminds us, in spirit at least, our yearning for discovery and the unknown being a possible reflection of this.

As well as being a journey into experiencing the world though the prism of other cultures, Griffiths' adventures also give us an insight into how the earliest Western explorers sought to conquer rather than to learn from the people they met – the legacy of that attitude is surely apparent in the language we use to describe our experiences of travel today. In her introduction, she writes:

> I wanted to live at the edge of the imperative, in the tender fury of the reckless moment, for in this brief and pointillist life, bright-dark and electric, I could do nothing else…For the human spirit has a primal allegiance to wildness, to really live, to snatch the fruit and suck it…

We're being urged to live in the moment again, though Griffiths experiences wildness not through self-destructive behaviour (what we often term wild behaviour), but by seeking knowledge outside her own experience.

She collects her journeys into four chapters based on the four elements of Ancient Greece – earth, air, fire and water – and visits places where wilderness can still be found: the jungle, the Arctic, mountains and desert. She writes of finding other ways of 'knowing' from the indigenous cultures she spends time in, at one point explaining that 'the Western way of knowing has denied validity to every mind save its own'. As she makes her way deeper and deeper into the jungle along the river and continues to take *ayahuasca*, this way of looking at the world becomes a flow of discovery that allows us all to glimpse a more intuitive way in which humans can make sense of their lives. Griffiths quotes a Native American who explains that in his culture, nature and the earth itself are seen as a library: their books are the birds, animals, trees and mountains. When his people want to think they lie on the earth to absorb its knowledge. All of which makes you wonder if our own landscape was once the source of unfathomable and wonderful ways of inhabiting the world.

Among indigenous cultures Griffiths frequently discovers the use of 'songlines' that enable the people she meets to travel in their landscape by singing songs that to an outsider seem almost magical. In his book *Songlines* Bruce Chatwin describes the Australian Aboriginals' 'labyrinth of invisible pathways which meander all over Australia'. The Aboriginal creation myths describe how the original beings of their culture literally 'sang' the world into existence; it is following their songlines, describing geographical aspects of the landscape, that allows them to journey hundreds of miles across what seem to Western eyes like almost featureless landscapes.

With deforestation in the Amazon jungle Griffiths discovers tribes who have lost their land, and with it the language of their culture, because it was tied intrinsically to their concept of the land. Having 'lost' their language they start to use the 'borrowed' language of the white man and quickly lose their sense of who they are and their connection with their ancestors. Griffiths tells us that over 300 of the Guarni-Kaiowa people in Brazil who lost their land and their language in this way committed suicide between 1986 and 1999. In deforestation we begin to see the destruction of knowledge as well as the loss of an ecosystem, which we in the West comfort ourselves into thinking can easily be replaced by a charitable donation. By needing to see this problem in a way that makes sense to us we're missing the reality, which Griffiths explains in graphic terms:

> In the Amazon, the assault against nature *is* an assault against culture, hundreds of tribal cultures. So burn their books, hack down their language and axe their philosophies. Tip Agent Orange into the eyes of a forest Picasso. Tie a Shakespeare's hands behind his back – with razor wire. Break Nureyev's ankles, stamp on Fonteyn's feet. Crack Joyce's head against a wall until the words whimper and fail him. Daub graffiti over an El Greco. Bulldoze the sculptures of Rodin...

Through her experiences we're being forced to look at our perceptions of the world in an entirely new way. This is the opposite end of the travel spectrum from the modern holiday. Discovering uncomfortable truths about the narrow focus of your own life is unsettling, but that is what travel is supposed to be. Griffiths' journeys are tough – she loses toenails through frostbite while scaling mountains, and she is forced to contend both with her own insecurities and with the blunt assessment of her by the people she meets along the way. In the Arctic she manages to persuade local hunters to let her on one of the boats heading out to hunt seals and whales. She can't suppress her physical revulsion when a seal is shot through the head at close range, despite supporting the right and need of the hunters to kill in order to survive. But this reaction results in her being left on land the next time they go to sea. She is angry with herself for appearing weak in front of them and realises how far removed her life has become from the wildness that others still rely on. Her experiences push her through bouts of terrible illness, too, but you can tell she wouldn't have it any other way.

Large sections of her book are spent analysing the language we use to reinforce the meaning behind the words that we use unthinkingly. Well, in *homage* to her, the word *travel* itself comes from the French word for work, *travaille*, which in turn originates from a Latin word *trepalium* – a three-pronged instrument of torture. As I said a moment ago, travel is *supposed* to be difficult. We're *supposed* to suffer, feel uncomfortable and put ourselves in danger if travel is what we are *really* looking for.

***

The contrast between travel as an intuitive means of discovering new ways of 'knowing' and the actions of those who embark on it with the calculated destruction of knowledge in mind is also examined in *Wild*. Stories of the appalling actions of missionaries and the death and destruction they bring to indigenous communities are painful to read. Griffiths tells the story of missionaries in Peru who competed to find 'uncontacted' tribes by roaring up river in helicopters. Their preferred method of bamboozling these unsuspecting people was to give them mirrors, which gave the impression they had supernatural powers and could make them feel they had been seen by the Christian God.

Griffiths points out that prior to seeing their own reflections in mirrors these tribal cultures had viewed the landscape as an extension of themselves. This symbolic act becomes the crack that ultimately enables the missionaries to split the people from their culture and their land.

After meeting a missionary family from Texas, Griffiths describes the look on their children's faces as having 'murderous incuriosity', as though their lack of hunger for other ways of thinking has made a wasteland of their own minds. The missionaries talk of saving people's souls but bring diseases that the tribe's traditional healers are unable to heal, which makes them lose faith in their own medicinal culture. Griffiths writes of a place called Itahuania in Peru. Once the missionaries were established there they built roads and the loggers came not long after. Now there is a white empty space in the forest where Itahuania used to be. In Ecuador, Texaco followed the missionaries. People Griffiths met from the Harakmbut tribe, also in Peru, told her that the diseases the missionaries brought (influenza, fever, measles) wiped out 50 per cent of their population. She writes: 'In South America as a whole, when a tribe's fate is known, between a third and a half of people have died within five years of first contact.' The most pertinent quote comes from an old Harakmbut man referred to as 'Tarzan', who remembers when they first came:

> No one wanted to go to school, and anyway after the missionaries came, our children died. We learned things, though: we learned money and Spanish and work. We learned that we had to work for money for needs we didn't have before…now we know we *lack* money, which we hadn't known we lacked before.

This is a painfully accurate assessment of a culture whose identity is predicated on the perceptions of the left hemisphere of the brain. When it's put like that, our Western concept of money and the global economy being the pinnacle of human progress begins to falter. The foundations on which we build our sense of identity and self-confidence are in danger of giving way. This is precisely the kind of challenge to the way we unquestioningly think about ourselves that travel is *supposed* to pose.

Sadly the missionaries are following many of the behaviours that were apparent in the earliest Western explorers. The dark side of the desire to travel can be found in the determination to conquer the furthest reaches of the globe, which resulted in the enslaving of millions in colonies. The act of mapping and surveying unknown (to the West anyway) parts of the globe was of scientific interest and pioneered the cataloguing of nature, but the information that came out of it was of great value to the burgeoning British Empire, and gave the military vital knowledge of how to invade and then how to expand their influence.

We must accept the legacy of that attitude in our own ideas about what it means to travel. Our 'Age of Discovery' led our ancestors to cultures for whom travel was a curse; in many instances this brought about their annihilation and, in Griffiths' words, 'a net reduction' in the knowledge of the world. This attitude still prevails in the continued acceptance of Western names for geographical features such as Mount Everest, which the Sherpas call 'Mother of long life'. Griffiths writes: 'Stripped of its identity as a female deity it was given the name of a male functionary, the surveyor-general of India, George Everest. From goddess to bureaucrat at a stroke of a pen.'

This kind of anti-travel, which destroys the very places we most longingly seek, is apparent in large parts of the tourist industry today. Vast swathes of the globe have had their indigenous cultures sanitised and wiped clean to make way for the homogenous brands that continue to spread into the farthest reaches of the planet. Griffiths finds solace in the wildness that was there before the developers came. She finds the reality of supermarkets and microwave ready meals far more threatening than the wildlife of any jungle and this seems to me to be the purpose of her book: to challenge our notion of what we think gives us security.

***

Griffiths' exploration of the way different cultures make sense of their own environment – and how radically different their perceptions are from our own – leads us to McGilchrist's conclusion about how the two hemispheres of the brain have impacted on human development. I find it hard to believe that my mind is capable of learning a song that would help me travel through the jungle or across the Australian outback, but this ability is hidden somewhere in my brain and could have been extracted if I had been brought up with another way of experiencing the world. But I don't have to be able to learn that song to get an inkling of how different my view of the world I live in would be, were I able to. What matters is being aware that other ways of 'knowing' exist, respecting them and doing what we can to protect them from the uniformity of the Western point of view.

Given the way the brain makes sense of the world, the different cultures and ways of 'knowing' that exist are surely what we're all ultimately looking for when we travel. Paradoxically, though, our own culture of searching has a tendency to obliterate everything in its path, which is why what we seek is often so hard to find. I'm convinced that when we travel we're looking for what we've forgotten just as much as what we don't know. Not as individuals, but as a species. We want to know who we are and where we came from. We want to *remember* where we came from and the different definitions of what it means to 'know'. That is possible, because that journey of discovery is held in the evolutionary structure of every human brain. Perhaps the urge to travel is an attempt to force us to remember what we are capable of, and this is the instinct behind the familiar line that travel can 'broaden the mind.'

***

McGilchrist argues that human development itself is a story of the battle between the left and right hemispheres of the brain. He suggests that while we live in a time when the perspective of the left hemisphere is in the ascendant, there have been societies in human history with a more balanced point of view. This too touches on the evolution of Western travel.

Prior to the Reformation in 16th-century England, when Henry VIII broke off from Rome to create the Protestant church (so he could 'legitimately' marry Anne Boleyn, whom he later beheaded), travel was largely tied to spiritual pilgrimage, which we'll look at in the last chapter. But once Britain was cut off from the Catholic continent it became very hard for Protestants to travel outside their own country. Going to Rome at the time would have been like an American going to Moscow at the height of the Cold War. To travel almost became an act of treachery, good Protestants knew their place and stayed at home.

With religious pilgrimage closed off, foreign travel had to redefine its purpose. While Italy was the centre of the Catholic Church, it was also the home of the Renaissance – literally a rebirth of interest in classical Greek and Roman ideas based around philosophy, literature and art. The Grand Tour emerged in the 17th century as a way for a small number of rich men to complete their education by touring the artworks, architecture and antiquities of a range of European cities, including Florence, Siena and Rome. Travel became an opportunity to cross over metaphorical and physical barriers, and the ideas these men encountered far from home led to a new appetite for self-discovery. There were reports and cartoons in London newspapers that questioned the patriotism of those who went abroad, but as most of these travellers were from the rich upper classes they could afford to do as they pleased.

James Howells' *Instructions for Foreign Travel*, published in 1642, details his thoughts and experiences of travelling through Europe from 1616 onwards, which he collates into a guide for those setting out on adventures of their own. He begins by extolling the virtues of the human eye, and explains how much more beneficial it is to travel and see things for yourself than it is to sit in stuffy rooms, poring over maps and listening to the travel stories of others. The ear, he says, offers 'weak and distrustful notions', while the eye has 'a more quick and immediate commerce and familiarity with the Soul' (the idea of the conscious mind and living in the moment once again). He writes of the benefits to be found through 'conversation with the dead', by which he means the writings of other men, most notably Homer's *Odyssey*. But he also encourages a balance between their ideas and the wisdom of your own mind, which you can access through witnessing each sight for yourself. There is a wonderful passage in which he explains it is only by travelling that you get a proper view of the heavens. If you remain in one place you see the same stars, which are beautiful and yet ordered and mundane, but as you move across the world you begin to see the greater complexity of the universe. Howells describes this as the 'genius of all active and generous spirits'. If there's a better metaphor for the way travel can change the way you think, I haven't come across it yet.

Howells' book is packed with ideas about travel, but my favourite passage relates to the importance of keeping a diary. Howells urges all his readers to become travel writers, and this is crucial in understanding the difference between the educational perspective of the

Grand Tour in the 17th century and the descent into vice and debauchery it had largely become by the end of the 18th. He writes that: '…the Pen makes the deepest furrows, and does fertilize, and enrich the memory more than anything else'. Perhaps this highlights what we miss in the act of recording our experiences when we take photographs today. In the future, notebooks filled with our thoughts and ideas will undoubtedly be more evocative of our travel experience than gigabytes of empty images.

Books on art that emerged as the Grand Tour became established acted as travel manuals for those who wanted to see specific paintings and sculptures of the Renaissance. The great country houses of England became museums reflecting the ideas people had been exposed to in Italy and France and provided a home for the collections they brought home from their travels. Landscape gardening and neoclassical architecture were born out of the act of seeing and being open to a different kind of culture and environment.

The upper classes soon knew far more about Italy and France than they did about Britain itself and certainly travelled through them much more extensively. A few were so inspired by the architecture they had seen that they re-created versions of them on their estates, some of which became the follies that we can still see scattered across the British countryside.

Edgar Allan Poe was fascinated by one of these men, a chap called William Beckford, who embarked on such a building programme and who epitomised the new direction that the Grand Tour was taking.

Beckford's estate at Fonthill in Wiltshire is mentioned in *The Domain of Arnheim* we encountered earlier and his life story has echoes of that of Poe's main character, Ellison, that are worth dwelling on here.

Beckford was born in 1760 and inherited his father's fortune – including £1 million in cash, the income of a number of West Indian sugar plantations, and the Fonthill estate – when he was only nine years old. Byron called him 'England's wealthiest son'. At 17 he was sent to Geneva, where he wrote his first book; he had completed his Grand Tour of France, Italy, Germany and Holland by the time he was 21. His travels allowed him to discover new ideas in a way that would have been much more difficult at home, and they would come to define him.

He had a homosexual affair in Venice and stayed with Lady Hamilton in Naples; she later wrote to warn him of the scandal he would face if he continued to succumb to such 'criminal passions'. He returned home for a lavish and opulent coming-of-age party at Fonthill. (The memory of this would inspire him to write his most famous and audacious work, *Vathek*, a gothic novel about an Arabian Caliph that recalled the wonder of the *Arabian Nights,* translated into English for the first time in 1706.) Beckford employed a theatrical set designer to transform the interior of his house for the occasion and was forbidden from entering for three days while the work took place. In the introduction to *Vathek* there is a note of what he encountered when he finally ventured in:

> The solid Egyptian Hall looked as if hewn out of a living rock—the line of apartments and apparently endless passages extending from it on either side were all vaulted—an interminable staircase, which when you looked down it appeared as deep as the well in the pyramid—and when you looked up was lost in vapour, led to suites of stately apartments gleaming with marble pavements—as polished as glass—and gawdy ceilings…the splendour of the gilded roofs—was partially obscured by the vapour of wood aloes ascending in wreaths from cassolettes placed low on the silken carpets in porcelain salvers of the richest Japan. The delirium of delight into which our young fervid bosoms were cast by such a combination of seductive influences may be conceived too easily.

Beckford described the new interior of his house as being like the 'Halls of Elbis', the evil Jinn, or Devil, from Islamic mythology (considering it was paid for off the back of slavery, he was perhaps closer to the truth than he knew).

A few months later, once *Vathek* had been completed, he was forced to flee the country in the wake of a scandal arising from a relationship he had with his cousin's wife. He then married and lived in Switzerland for a while, before returning to become a Member of Parliament. That was short-lived, too: the press uncovered more scandal and he took himself off to Switzerland again. By this stage he had reached the grand old age of 24. He continued to travel extensively in the years that followed, writing travel books while living in Paris, Lisbon and Madrid, and returning occasionally to plan the building of the vast Fonthill Abbey that would be both his greatest achievement and his greatest folly. Enough work had been done on the abbey by 1800 for Beckford to entertain Lord Nelson and Lady Hamilton in it, but it was not completed until 1809. It collapsed 15 years later – after he'd sold it and turned his attention to other follies in Bath.

Beckford was ostracised by polite society and epitomised for many the worst excesses of the idle rich, but he was a man of his age, defined by his travel experiences and, because of his inheritance, able to act out the impulses stemming from an almost limitless appetite for excess. He was a Renaissance man in the sense that he placed himself at the centre of his own universe and pursued his curiosity wherever it led. He indulged all four of Poe's conditions of bliss: travel, love, the contempt of ambition (his failed career as an MP and a later failed attempt to become a member of the House of Lords were at the behest of his family rather than himself) and the pursuit of his own creativity in his immense collections of books and paintings and his various eccentric building programmes. He was able to blend the life of reality and imagination in a form that Poe would later wrestle with in creating Ellison and his quest to refine the world according to his own point of view.

***

So what was it about the Grand Tour and the works of the Italian Renaissance that could alter the attitude to life of those who were able to experience it and act on what they discovered?

As we saw earlier, McGilchrist suggests that the different perceptions of the left and right hemispheres of the brain account for the way we live, and that we have become dominated by the left hemisphere's preference for structure and order. He argues that this is evident in our Western culture, which is designed and focused around measurable, quantifiable things. The British government's emphasis on the economy, bureaucracy, league tables, testing, surveillance and the constant push to evolve technology all stem from the left hemisphere's ordered point of view. The intuitive, creative mind, open to new ways of thinking, that Jay Griffiths experienced in other cultures, hardly gets a look-in these days. And if it does, its value is arguably determined only after it has been commoditised – converted into an ordered system – by the industries that grow up around creative spirits.

In the second half of his book, McGilchrist suggests that the left brain's dominance of society has not always been this way and gives two examples of societies in human history where the left and right hemispheres of the brain were more balanced. As a result they inspired a very different outlook. If you haven't guessed by now, they were Athens around the fifth century BC and Italy in the 15th and 16th, during the Renaissance, or 're-birth', of Athenian ideas.

The Renaissance was directly inspired by a way of thinking rediscovered from Ancient Greece that would radically change the Western world. The attraction of these ideas that manifested itself in the Grand Tour became the blueprint of the way we viewed travel in the secular West – as an exercise in personal enrichment and discovery. One example of the balance of the two hemispheres of the brain evident in the Ancient Greeks' world-view is surely the approach to time that we've already come across. The fact that they were able to value and appreciate both Chronos and Kairos is evidence to me that their perceptions of life were far more balanced than ours today. I don't know about you, but I long to live in a society that places *equal* value on the time of order *and* the time of our lives.

The leaders of the Renaissance were all imbued with a new concept of the self; they came to terms with themselves through introspection and the search for how they could live better lives and become better people, rather than by taking part in rituals to please an external, supernatural power. This concept became known as humanism and it spread through ideas that emerged from the teachings of Cicero, the Roman philosopher who himself followed the works of great thinkers from Ancient Greece. As many of the most influential proponents of humanism were Christian, this resulted in the evolution of the church along humanist lines too. The 'humanist' education that emerged from the Renaissance has evolved into the 'humanities' today – the academic study of the human condition; the classics, languages, literature, history, philosophy, religion, social sciences, arts, anthropology – all of which acknowledge the importance of the right hemisphere of the brain. From about the 15th century, the widening of education to include these areas of study became the crucible from which ideas and creativity would explode into a beacon for the travelling, enquiring minds of Europe to follow. Perhaps it's too neat, but it's tantalising to imagine that the urge to travel itself was reborn as a secular pilgrimage in search of the very balance that McGilchrist attributes to the perceptions and priorities of both hemispheres of the brain – as epitomised by the Renaissance.

Whether or not that is still the case, even if it was then, the left hemisphere's perception of the world, and its need for order, has undoubtedly got out of hand in the Western world today. At the time of writing, the humanities subjects that were supported with such energy during the Renaissance are the very areas suffering the greatest cuts in funding in UK universities – precisely *because* their value is so hard to measure and explain and cannot be accounted for as easily as the scientific and practical subjects that please the left hemisphere's world view. The left hemisphere's approach to travel seems unassailable, too. By turning the world into a catalogue of predictable, inevitable experiences which rely on little input from our minds, we've forgotten the impulse that urges us to move in the first place: the desire to redefine how we see our own lives by being confronted by the unknown, and in the process discover new definitions of what it means to 'know'.

[illegible]

Be [illegible]

[illegible]

[illegible] the Ultra [illegible]

[illegible]

[illegible] screen, but it was a phenomen[illegible]

[illegible] me. She had only the [illegible]

Chapter 7

Be epic

We have become human doings rather than human beings.
Slow down, you'll go further than you've ever imagined.
Satish Kumar, No Destination

I went to the Uffizi Gallery in Florence a few years ago to see a pair of Renaissance paintings called the *Duke and Duchess of Urbino* by Piero della Francesca, which I had seen before when Henry and I visited the city when we were both 19. I'm not a religious person, but these paintings have become something of a pilgrimage for me. Not because I'm a huge fan of the pictures themselves, which I know very little about, but because I intend to visit them in each decade of my life.

The first time I was made aware of Piero's masterpiece it was a black and white projection on the wall of an art-history class during my first failed attempt at university. The seminar room was too small for the number of students it contained and the teacher did her best to inspire us about the image on the makeshift screen, but it was a 'phonetic' experience and wasn't for me. She had only the image of the Duke; the Duchess was nowhere to be seen. I dropped out a few weeks later. One thing the teacher said stuck with me, though – that your response to a painting tells you more about you than about the work of art itself.

When I stood in front of both paintings with Henry 12 months later I smiled a knowing smile. Working in a series of tedious jobs to earn enough money for the trip had been a struggle, but it had been worth it in the end. Extracting myself from that seminar and following the hunch that I should go and see the paintings for real created a meaning that the artist could never have intended. It sounds pretentious (I was 19, remember), but I felt as if the process of getting myself in front of those paintings had drawn the art of life from me. I was full of the hopes of what my life would turn out like and who I would turn out to be. Henry and I were staying in a campsite on a hill outside the city. I was wearing a rucksack, trying to grow a beard and clutching a notebook in which I'd written reams of terrible poetry. The plan to leave Higher Education had been widely condemned by everyone closest to me, but standing in front of the paintings gave me confidence that it had been the right decision. It was a moment of triumph. As I left, I promised myself I would come back and see them again throughout my life to remind myself to follow my instincts rather than the sensible path that supposedly offered security.

On that second visit 12 years later I was with Rachel and Wilf, who was toddling at the time, on a work trip for a newspaper. As Wilf insisted on charging around the gallery I didn't have much time to look at the paintings. I stood in front of the Duke and Duchess for a few minutes and looked at the other visitors spilling around me. There is a window to the left of them and my eye was drawn outside. I thought back over the years since I'd seen them and last stared out at that scene. I picked Wilf up to show him the paintings but it was my dream, not his, and he wriggled away quickly.

This is not an exercise in nostalgia, more a way of reminding myself of the ideas that have guided me throughout my life – most of which I'm now convinced originate from the right hemisphere of my brain. When Ian came up with the idea of driving across England in a milk float, for example, and I had an intuitive sense that we should go for it, I smiled at the memory of my 19-year-old self standing in that gallery. The other intriguing aspect to it – that only occurred to me while writing this book – is that it turns the concept of travel entirely on its head. The paintings are still a destination, of course, but by revisiting them I turn my life in between visits into a series of decade-long journeys. All of which helps me think of my whole life as a travel experience, rather than just those chunks of time we call the annual holiday. And while it might be ridiculous to imagine the modern-day tourist as an updated version of Odysseus, we *are* nevertheless all Odysseus when it comes to our individual lives. For me, this is why slow travel is so compelling, because you begin to think about your life as the only epic reality you will ever truly inhabit.

Our existence is a narrative constructed through the experience of our own memory and the future we imagine in front of us. We think of ourselves through the medium of a story: where we came from, the early experiences that define the way we look at our lives and the choices we make that send us onto a specific path. We are all the authors of our own experience, which is why it's so important to stop and look around occasionally. If you allow yourself to be funnelled into a series of 'phonetic' experiences, ticking off one box after another, life flies by very quickly.

The psychologist Claudia Hammond examines this idea in her book *Time Warped,* which looks at the way we experience time as our lives progress. She quickly debunks the popular perception that life seems to move faster as we get older simply because a year in the life of a five-year-old is a greater portion of their entire existence than it is for a 50-year-old. This is not true. If it were, each individual day of our lives would seem to speed up as we age, which it does not. Instead, Hammond argues that the way we experience time depends entirely on what we *do* with our time. The more we move away from our regular routine, and the more conscious we are of what we're doing, the more slowly time seems to pass.

This is something I have noticed on my own travels. By the time I get home from any slow travel journey I feel as though I've been away for far longer than the number of hours, days or weeks that are shown on a watch or a calendar. The trip Kev and I went on to Mull is a good example. By the time we arrived back in London on the Monday morning it felt as though we'd been away for weeks, not four days. I'm sure it's because we were living consciously, rather than unconsciously, for the entire duration of the trip. If you want your life to slow down and not race away from you, you have to live in the moment and engage with it completely. In doing so, your life really does become an adventure you can revel in, rather than a conveyor belt of routine that will rush you towards your very final breath.

When you think about it, we do seem to spend much more time worrying about how we can prolong our life span rather than improving the quality of that life, as though extending our life in measurable terms were far more important that the lives we actually lead. Life, like travel, is not really about distance. It's the *depth* of your experience that counts and, just as the length of the coast of Britain depends entirely on the way you measure it, so it is with life itself. The more deeply you engage with life, the longer it will seem to be.

This philosophy is encapsulated in the Slow Food movement – a campaign launched by Carlo Petrini as a protest against the opening of a branch of McDonald's by the Spanish Steps in Rome. What started as a desire to promote local and ethical produce as an alternative to the fast-food culture soon became the focal point for an entire life philosophy. 'Slow' events have subsequently popped up all over the world and embraced a variety of subjects, from Slow Gardening to Slow Parenting. I'm not connected with the organisation myself, but I see its growing popularity as an early sign of a new way of thinking spreading across the world, pushing for a more balanced focus than the one that has dominated the way we live for so long. We certainly should be open to it after the financial meltdown of our recent history.

***

If anyone can teach us to think of our own lives in deeper terms it is Satish Kumar. His autobiography is called, appropriately for our purposes, *No Destination*. If Petrini is the father of the slow movement, then Kumar must be its deity – although he would no doubt brush that thought away with a kind but baffled curiosity.

Kumar was born in Sri Dungargarh, Rajasthan, in the north of India, in 1936. His father died suddenly when he was four and the shock of seeing his corpse persuaded the young boy to become a wandering Jain monk five years later. The Jain order believes in non-violence to an extreme degree. The monks wear a piece of gauze across their face to prevent any risk of injuring insects that might fly into their mouths. They walk staring at the earth to make sure no living creature is crushed by their footsteps and brush the ground before they sit down to ensure they don't harm anything. In this voluntary life sentence, Kumar was also forbidden from using any form of transport other than his own two feet. He spent the next nine years walking thousands of miles barefoot across India, learning to recite passages of sacred texts, meditating and giving talks; his only possessions were a begging bowl for food and the cloth that covered his body. He wasn't allowed to wash, either.

Then, when he was 18, he came across the writings of Gandhi. These persuaded him that in order to change the world you must be a part of it, rather than renounce it completely. Kumar concluded that the life he had lived as a monk was an extreme form of hiding. Before he left the Jain order – which he had to do clandestinely – he told the assembled followers in the village a story. In his autobiography he recalls the last words he spoke as a monk:

> We are all on a journey. It is a hard and dangerous journey. We must listen to the inner cry that disturbs the sleep. This inner cry is the source of salvation. Let me warn you that no outside authority can lead you to liberation…Even monks in their white robes can deceive themselves by blindly following the outer manifestations of the spiritual life, and by deceiving themselves they deceive everyone.

He escaped late that night and went in search of one of Gandhi's followers, Vinoba Bhave, who was making his own pilgrimage across India to persuade rich landowners to give up parts of their estates to the poorest sufferers of the caste system. Kumar joined one of Bhave's ashram communities and found that its purpose was a point of balance he'd been looking for. The principles of the ashram were 'to find a synthesis between the intellectual and the manual, between the head and the hands, between contemplation and action, and between science and spirituality'. Kumar began to accompany Bhave on his journeys across India, joining what Bhave referred to as a 'walking university'. He told Kumar not to get stuck and to 'keep flowing'.

In 1962, when he was 25, Kumar found his opportunity to flow and take action on the world stage when he read about the then 90-year-old British philosopher Bertrand Russell, who had just been imprisoned for his part in an anti-nuclear demonstration in London. Kumar was in a café and recalls saying to his friend Prabhakar: 'Here is a man of ninety committing civil disobedience and going to jail. What are we doing?'

They decided to embark on an epic pilgrimage, walking from Gandhi's grave to the capital cities of the four countries that had nuclear weapons – Moscow, Paris, London and Washington DC – to campaign against the nuclear threat. They began to raise money from friends and supporters to finance their journey before visiting Bhave to get his support. He greeted their idea warmly, telling them they would have his blessing as long as they took two weapons with them. Surprised to hear a fierce proponent of non-violence telling them to take weapons, they asked him to explain. He told them: 'The first weapon is that you will remain vegetarian in all circumstances; the second is that you will carry no money, not a single penny.' They agreed and he sent them on their way with a prediction that the world would meet them with open arms.

I find the logic of the second of those two weapons astonishing in its power and simplicity. Kumar later reflected in an interview that as it is fear that leads to war, trust must lead to peace; it made perfect sense to embark on a pilgrimage of peace that relied on the goodwill of complete strangers. We had money on our trip across England, but we relied on the trust of people we'd never met to help us charge the milk float. This led ultimately to the most meaningful and inspiring aspects of our journey – and we never paid for any electricity. We learned that if you have to rely on other people you are forced to be open and engage with them, which quickly spreads the notion of friendship and community. One person leads you to another further along your path or pushes you in a slightly different direction from the one you were imagining. It is a loss of control but an entirely life-affirming and liberating one. The power of that kind of behaviour as it spreads away from you is exponential.

If, on the other hand, you have plenty of money and no need of anyone's help, you can venture all over the world without meeting a single local person except for the ones who serve you – which is more or less where we've got to with the modern holiday.

***

The two pilgrims' journey started well as they travelled north through India. They were inundated with offers of food and places to stay, but their friends and supporters were terrified of what would happen to them when they crossed the border into Pakistan. One woman offered them a huge parcel of food, but Kumar and Prabhakar refused it, reasoning that to take it would be to imply that they mistrusted the Pakistani people. When they eventually went through customs they found a man who had heard about their pilgrimage on the radio and had been waiting for hours to ask them to come to his home.

Even in the most dangerous places such as the Khyber Pass in Afghanistan, where they feared for their own safety, they found the same generosity. An armed Pathan told them: 'Much malicious propaganda is made against us...Consequently we feel ignored and isolated. We believe that if a guest comes, God comes in him.'

In Iran they met the Shah, who supported their endeavour and tried to give them money; when they refused he laughed and said: 'We are the same. I also never carry money! The Shah and the *fakir* [a begging Muslim monk] meet on the same ground.' But he ensured they were treated well all the way to the Soviet border.

After 40 days of walking through Russia, they came to in a village in Armenia where they met two young women who worked in a tea factory. After hearing about the pilgrimage, one of the women disappeared and came back with four packets of tea. She told them, 'These are not for you. Please give one to our Premier in Moscow, one to the President of France, one to the Prime Minister of England and one to the President of the United States of America,' before urging them to tell the world leaders that if they ever found themselves in a position where they even contemplated pressing the nuclear button they must stop, make a cup of tea and remember all the ordinary people in the world who 'want bread, not bombs'.

Bread is a subject I've heard Kumar talk about on the radio. Through it he explains his philosophy that everything in life is improved if you are prepared to give it the gift of your own time. You cannot rush the baking of bread any more than you can rush the act of writing poetry. If you're prepared to face the truth of this, you'll find it applies to everything that has any meaning in your life. Friendships, relationships, parenting, something you build or plant with your hands, creative work, medical care, education and, of course, travel. Time is more valuable than money could ever dream of being, and yet the urge to speed us up and chase financial wealth is everywhere. The idea of time being a gift is very powerful, too. When you think about it in terms of your life as a whole, giving someone your time is the ultimate act of generosity.

Kumar and Prabhakar were eventually hoodwinked into flying to Moscow by the authorities, who were nervous about peace campaigners walking through the Soviet countryside. They did their best to protest, but were persuaded that they would achieve more by carrying their pilgrimage further into Europe than by being held in a Soviet prison. After passing through Poland they came to the border with East Berlin, just before President Kennedy's visit. Here they were interrogated by German and Russian soldiers – Kumar remembers how the men performed their duties 'mechanically and without heart'. After listening with grim faces to them talk about their adventures, one of the soldiers blurted out: 'You are right. We have no peace of mind here, at home or at the front. We are longing for the day when we can throw away these arms and join you in the fight for peace.'

They ended up in prison when they reached Paris, however, after taking part in an anti-nuclear demonstration outside the French President's palace. They were so horrified by the squalor of their cell that they went on hunger strike for three days. It had taken 16 months to walk to Paris but the French government told them they would be deported back to Delhi by aeroplane in 16 hours' time. In the end they agreed to be sent to Dover, from where they walked to London before being whisked away in a car to Snowdonia to meet the inspiration for their journey, Bertrand Russell.

Kumar was clearly impressed, recalling Russell as 'small in body yet giant in stature, old in age and young in courage, weak in limbs and strong in action...' Russell was concerned about how they would make their way to Washington and organised a fund-raising campaign to buy both men tickets for a passage to New York on the luxurious *Queen Mary*. Kumar wrote: 'Thanks to Vinoba's weapons, we were travelling in style.'

They walked from London to Southampton and sailed for America on 22 November 1963. Later that day President Kennedy was assassinated, and the 8,000-mile pilgrimage that had started at Gandhi's grave ended well over a year later, in January 1964, at Kennedy's tomb in Arlington, Virginia.

In his book Kumar reflects on the desolation he and Prabhakar felt when they finally arrived, having walked from the grave of one man killed by an assassin's bullet to another. Extraordinary and inspiring as their journey had been, their hope of spreading the message of peace seemed to have ended in failure. They had successfully delivered their packets of tea to the leaders of each nuclear power, but not to those leaders in person. In each case they had been received warmly, but told a variation on the same theme – that if only the 'other' country were to give up nuclear weapons then so would they. Kumar felt the same sensation in the corridors of power in each country:

> I found fear in Moscow and fear in Washington, fear in Paris and fear in London. The enemy is neither Russia nor America. It is fear which is the enemy of twentieth-century civilisation…eight thousand miles and eighteen months of walk ended in the bureaucratic defence of fear.

But they did meet someone who would inspire them: Martin Luther King invited them to visit just after he had delivered his 'I have a dream…' speech in Washington. In his house the two pilgrims found a large picture of Gandhi on the wall and King told them: 'My non-violence is a revolutionary non-violence, touching the deepest corners of human consciousness. I am convinced we will win.'

Kumar – the wandering Indian holy man – was part of the zeitgeist of change in popular culture in the USA and Europe in the 1960s and '70s, as a lack of access to the political process led youth movements to seek new ideas, just as Zweig and his contemporaries had sought fresh ways of thinking in Vienna over half a century earlier. Demonstrations against the Vietnam

War, the Czech and Slovak people protesting against Communism, and the fight for civil rights were meshed with the areas of life over which the young did have some control, in the form of music, art and culture – involving the right hemisphere of the brain once again. From that yearning for a new way to live, the East became the place many Westerners went to 'find themselves', which they often achieved through a combination of psychedelic drugs and meditation.

I've lost count of the number of cultural references I've come across and people I've met who have come back from India having embraced meditation (and sometimes drugs) and seem to 'see' possibilities for change that are counter-intuitive to the left hemisphere's ordered perception of the world. Not only do these people see possibilities, they act with a profound sense of commitment, against seemingly unassailable odds, to tackle unfairness in the world. A few years ago I wrote a book about political protesters in the UK who were finding themselves the target for arrest through laws that had been passed to tackle terrorism. In one notable example, Tony Blair's government passed legislation that prevented anyone holding a political demonstration within a thousand metres of the Houses of Parliament without prior permission from the police.

The use of anti-terrorist powers to curb freedom of speech was the same triumph of fear over democracy that Kumar had found on his pilgrimage – and the polar opposite of what all democratic governments are granted political power in order to protect. Yet these protesters were utterly unfazed by the scale of the challenge they faced. They were all convinced they could enact change and build a better future. A large number of them were 'hippie' types, imbued with a fresh sense of idealism based around community, co-operation, non-violence – all very reminiscent of Kumar's ideas, and very little to be seen in politicians today. They were often accused of being unrealistic, but Kumar had an answer for that, pointing out the pain and suffering in the world for which the realists were responsible. Many of the protesters I met had embraced meditation in spiritual communities as a way to explore the fabric of their existence, even if they hadn't travelled to the East themselves. This has become something of a cliché, but there is clearly something enticing about aspects of Eastern culture that we don't come across in our own. Perhaps these different ways of looking at the world are what continue to inspire many to head east in our modern version of the Grand Tour – the gap year.

Kumar eventually settled in Britain and became the editor of a magazine called *Resurgence,* whose aims are to spread the idea of ecological humanism. He began to apply practical ideas that he had developed through his spiritual journey of non-violence and wandering. He set up a school which placed equal value on philosophy, practical skills and academic study; it even introduced classes on silence. Kumar continues to be a beacon for new ideas at the helm of *Resurgence* and in his work for the Schumacher College, which is where I first came across a talk by a certain psychiatrist, philosopher and author called Iain McGilchrist.

Kumar's epic attitude to life continues to this day. He still embarks on pilgrimages, and walked between the major holy sites of Britain, again with no money, when he was 50. He is an inspiration to anyone who feels restricted by the kind of pessimistic realism that prevents many people from following their instincts or their dreams. The title of his book hints at the wider message contained in his philosophy, which applies beyond the idea of travel and into life itself: it doesn't matter where or what the ultimate destination of your life is, it's what you do with your time in between – the journey – that counts.

Kumar has described walking as meditation, and he would know. The dictionary definition of meditate is 'to exercise the mind in contemplation'. Contemplate means 'to survey with the eyes or with the mind'. For me, slow travel is a meditation based on a profound sense of curiosity, finding new ways to see the world and challenging your sense of what it means to 'know'. As with everything we experience in our lives, it relies entirely on the workings of our own brain, which is why I have spent as much time in this book trying to understand those workings as I have on travel itself. Whether travel really takes place in physical movement or simply in the mind, human beings have been on a journey of discovery since they first felt the urge to leave Africa and spread out across the world.

Today the internet is changing the way we travel in all kinds of ways that help the idle traveller. In February 2012, the UK travel agent Thomas Cook announced the closure of 200 high-street branches and, while the loss of jobs is always a sad thing, it gives me a sense of optimism that people are beginning to take control of their travel experiences once more. It's now possible for anyone to organise their own adventures with a little bit of research, and with new platforms like airbnb.com – which allows people across the world to offer their homes, spare rooms or even their sofas to travellers for a reasonable fee – you get the best of both worlds, as the local knowledge of your host comes free of charge. These might be small changes, but they open up extraordinary possibilities.

***

My own passion for travel was passed down to me by an incredibly inspiring woman called Rita, who also happened to be my Granny: visiting where she used to live is another recurring pilgrimage I go on occasionally. She spent 30 years in the same flat in Fishbourne, which she chose because of the view across the harbour you could see from its balcony. She died a few years ago, but I often walk there and potter over the bridges where we played pooh-sticks when I was a small boy. Her ashes were spread among the reeds and, because I enjoyed so many wonderful times in her company, arriving there always feels like coming home. She was a nurse during the Second World War and afterwards moved with her husband John to the place in southern England furthest away from his childhood home in Ireland and hers in Lincolnshire. In Chichester they worked together at a hospital that has now been converted into a complex of luxury homes.

Having toiled and saved all their lives they planned to see the world together when they retired, but when John died suddenly it seemed that their dream had gone. No one would have blamed Rita for collapsing into a pit of grief, but she decided to go for both of them. She spent the next 30 years travelling the world on her own. Throughout my childhood she always seemed to be heading off on intrepid adventures on the other side of the world, and my brother Gareth and I would revel in the exotic treats she brought back with her when she finally came home. She had found a way of channelling her grief into a new form of love for the unknown, and often used to tell me 'to get out there and *live* in the world' as soon as I had the opportunity.

As well as presents, she also came back with postcards, aeroplane food menus, museum brochures and anything else she had used during her stay that she thought two small boys might enjoy. I remember being mesmerised by these obscure pieces of paper far more than by the gifts she gave us – Egyptian bus tickets, brochures in Chinese from Hong Kong, restaurant bills from the Caribbean – but mostly Gareth and I would just sit down and listen to her tell us stories about her travels and the ideas she'd discovered from the places she'd been. We adored her and hung on her every word, especially when she furnished us with crisps and turned the lights off in the lounge to talk us through the slides from her latest expedition.

When I was a teenager she started to take me with her on Wallace Arnold coach tours across Europe, and once to Ireland to visit the birthplace of the grandfather

I never knew. I was usually the youngest person on the coach by a good 50 years, and I look a little odd in the collection of photographs I have of everyone posing in front of the coach on the last morning of a trip, but I treasure those memories today. As we sat side by side for hours driving through Europe she would tell me about her many experiences and I was honoured to be her companion. Her favourite place was Machu Picchu in Peru, which she scaled when she was in her 70s after going down the Rio Urubamba in a canoe. She told me the guide had given her cocoa leaves to chew to stave off altitude sickness; they had been so energising that she had brought a fair few home. I was aghast, and told her that the leaves were the basis of cocaine and she could have been arrested. She tapped my knee and said, 'I was a nurse for thirty years, you know'. Then, staring out the window, she added nonchalantly, 'Customs never bother searching the bags of doddery old ladies, anyway'.

***

It was on those trips that I first began to understand what travel is capable of distilling if you go beyond the anaesthetic of more conventional holiday experiences. Rita didn't just talk of her travels as we sat on those ferries, trains and coaches, she began to tell me more about her life and what it had been like to work as a nurse when the Second World War began. She also had a sideline as a kind of chauffeur for two of her friends who toured Britain's golf and race courses in the 1970s and '80s. They had an enormous Rolls-

Royce and Granny drove it and them everywhere, peering over the enormous steering wheel and later finding herself seated next to famous jockeys and golfers at dinner in glamorous hotels.

It's hard to explain the effect it had on me as a child to have a little old Granny who thought nothing of doing this kind of thing, although I like to think you can see an echo of her in my own seemingly eccentric attitude to life and travel. She said I reminded her of my grandfather, but more than anything I wanted to be like her. In my mind I can still hear her chatting away, and whenever I travel, on every bus, train and ferry, I smile at the empty seat beside me…

Epilogue

I finished writing this book on a Monday morning and plodded downstairs with a combined sense of exhaustion and relief. I was greeted by Olive standing in the lounge at the bottom of the stairs. In the time it has taken me to write this, she has begun to talk much more fluently. She dived into my legs to give me a hug and I bent over and kissed the top of her head. She looked up expectantly, said, 'Shoes, Daddy' and then sat on the floor, wiggling her toes. I stepped around her and eventually found her boots under the sofa. Once I'd zipped them on she stood up and turned to me. 'Walk, Daddy.' It was not a question. She was off through the gate before I'd made it out of the front door.

Bibliography

The author and publisher would like to thank the following for allowing or not raising objections to the use of copyright material: *Zweig, Journeys*, translated by Will Stone, Hesperus Press, 2010. *WILD* by Jay Griffiths (Hamish Hamilton 2007) copyright © Jay Griffiths. *The Horse Boy* by Rupert Isaacson (Viking 2009) copyright © Rupert Isaacson. *No Destination* by Satish Kumar, published by Green Books copyright © Satish Kumar. *As I Walked Out One Midsummer Morning* (Penguin 1971) copyright © Laurie Lee (Estate). *Vathek* (Oxford World's Classics) by William Beckford and Roger Lonsdale (1998), by permission of Oxford University Press. 'The Whitsun Weddings' taken from *Collected Poems* © Estate of Philip Larkin and reprinted by permission of Faber and Faber Ltd

Peter Ackroyd, *Blake,* Vintage, 1999
William Beckford, *Vathek,* Oxford World Classics, 1998
James Boswell, *Johnson's Journey to the Hebrides*, Philip Allan & Co, 1925
Bruce Chatwin, *In Patagonia,* Vintage, 1998
—— *The Songlines,* Vintage, 1998
—— *What Am I Doing Here?,* Vintage, 2005
Mark Cocker, *Loneliness and Time,* Secker & Warburg, 1992
Roger Deakin, *Notes From Walnut Tree Farm,* Penguin, 2009
David Eagleman, *Incognito,* Canongate, 2011
Patrick Leigh Fermor, *Words of Mercury,* John Murray, 2003
Frederick Forsyth, *The Day of the Jackal,* Hutchinson, 1971
Jay Griffiths, *Wild: An Elemental Journey,* Hamish Hamilton, 2006
Claudia Hammond, *Time Warped*, Canongate, 2012

William Hazlitt, *On Going A Journey*, *The New Monthly Magazine*, 1822
Miroslav Holub, *Brief Thoughts On Maps*, *The Literary Times Supplement*, 1977
Rupert Isaacson, *The Horse Boy,* Vintage, 2009
John Keane, *Vaclav Havel,* Bloomsbury, 1999
Satish Kumar, *No Destination,* Green Books, Devon, 2004
Philip Larkin, *Collected Poems*, Faber & Faber, 1990
Lao Tzu, *Tao Te Ching,* Frances Lincoln, 1999
Laurie Lee, *As I Walked Out One Midsummer Morning,* Penguin, 1973
Dean MacCannell, *The Tourist*, Shocken Books, 1976
Benoît Mandelbrot 'How Long Is the Coast of Britain? Statistical Self-Similarity and Fractional Dimension', *Science,* New Series, Vol. 156, No. 3775 (5 May 1967)
Iain McGilchrist, *The Master and His Emissary,* Yale University Press, 2010
H V Morton, *I Saw Two Englands,* Methuen, 1947
Andrew Newberg & Mark Robert Waldman, *How God Changes Your Brain,* Ballantine, 2010
Edgar Allan Poe, *Tales of Mystery and Imagination,* Everyman, 1998
Justin Pollard, *Seven Ages of Britain* Hodder & Stoughton, 2005
Jonathan Raban, *Coasting* Picador, 1987
Carl E Schorske *Fin-de-Siècle Vienna,* Vintage, 1980
W G Sebald, *The Rings of Saturn,* Vintage, 2002
Jill Bolte Taylor, *My Stroke of Insight,* Hodder & Stoughton, 2009
Paul Theroux, *Ghost Train to the Eastern Star,* Hamish Hamilton, 2008
Henry David Thoreau, *Walden,* Penguin Classics, 1986
Travel Writing 1700 –1830, Oxford World Classics, 2008
The Upanishads, Penguin Classics, London, 1965
Semir Zeki, *Splendours and Miseries of the Brain,* Wiley & Blackwell, 2009
Stefan Zweig, *Journeys,* Hesperus, 2010 *The World of Yesterday*, Plunkett Lake Press, 2011

Index

Acknowledgements

It may seem a little odd, but the thing I am most indebted to for revealing the joys of slow travel is my fear of flying. Every person I've ever met has told me I must get over this fear, but I have always tried to make a virtue of failure. I now realise that it is my inability to fly that forced me to think about what it really means to travel. Without it I'm not sure I would ever have discovered how to travel at all.

On a more practical note, Helen Brocklehurst's determination to publish a book on this subject is what made it happen. These thoughts and ideas have been drifting around my head for two decades but it was only after talking to her that it occurred to me to try to put them into a book. I am also very grateful to Tom Hodgkinson, who was originally supposed to write it but who passed the opportunity to me because he knew the subject was close to my heart.

Writing a book while launching a new business was always going to be tricky, and I only managed it thanks to support and illuminating conversations with my friends at Unbound, Justin Pollard, Isobel Frankish, John Mitchinson, Xander Cansell, Caitlin Harvey and Christoph Sander. My parents were also very generous with their time and conversation and leapt at every opportunity to help take care of the children.

Finally, I would like to thank Rachel, Olive and Wilf. Ultimately, it is their patience and support that allows me to do what I love. This summer we're renting a house for a week near a beach where the sun is guaranteed to shine. We're also doing a 12-day trip to Marrakesh, by ferry and overnight train.